THE
BLACK
HUMANIST
EXPERIENCE

THE
BLACK
HUMANIST
EXPERIENCE

An Alternative to Religion

Edited by

NORM R. ALLEN JR.

 **Prometheus Books**

59 John Glenn Drive
Amherst, New York 14228-2197

Published 2003 by Prometheus Books

Inquiries should be addressed to
Prometheus Books
59 John Glenn Drive
Amherst, New York 14228–2197
VOICE: 716–691–0133, ext. 207
FAX: 716–564–2711
WWW.PROMETHEUSBOOKS.COM

07 06 05 04 03   5 4 3 2 1

Library of Congress Cataloging-in-Publication Data
The Black humanist experience : an alternative to religion / edited by Norm R. Allen Jr.
        p. cm.
Includes bibliographical references.
ISBN 1–57392–967–0 (alk. paper)
    1. Humanism, Religious. 2. African Americans—Religion. I. Allen, Norm R.

BL2747.6 .B54 2002
211'.6'08996073—dc21

2002068087

Printed in the United States of America on acid-free paper

CONTENTS

Introduction
Norm R. Allen Jr.   9

1. Millennial Apocalypse: A Street Preacher's View
Franz Vanderpuye   15

2. Humanism, Reason, and Emotion
Leonard Harris   23

3. My Journey from Catholicism to Humanism
Carolyn M. Dejoie   31

4. Living on the Threshold of Magnificence:
An Autobiographical Essay
Ranjini L. Thaver   37

5. A Believer's Testimony
   Igwe Ucheakolam   43

6. A Secular and Religious Gumbo, Served Brown
   Kenyatta Yamel   47

7. "My Lord, I Want to Go and Think"
   (Choosing Reason Over Faith)
   Leo Igwe   53

8. Ascension to Humanism
   Keenya H. Oliver   59

9. Thinking Back
   Anthony B. Pinn   67

10. From Supernaturalism to Agnosticism
    David Stewart Summers   73

11. The Catholic Education of an Atheist
    Patrick Inniss   79

12. My Long and Winding Road to Humanism
    Nkeonye Otakpor   89

13. How I Became an Atheist
    Gebregeorgis Yohannes   99

14. Salvation through Education
    Dominic I. Ogbonna   105

15. Rebel with a Cause
    Micah Lamptey   111

16. Praying My Way toward Humanism
    David Allen   115

17. Embracing the Power of Humanism
    Gladman C. Humbles   119

18. From Christianity to Sanity
    Anthony Burnside   123

19. Making an Easy and Natural Transition
    Chaka Ferguson   127

20. Reflections on Religion and Humanism
    Charles W. Faulkner   131

21. Crossing the Border in a Golden Search:
    A Testimony on Personal Enlightenment
    Alfred T. Kisubi   135

22. The Black Humanist Experience:
    An Alternative to Religion
    Norm R. Allen Jr.   147

Contributors   165

INTRODUCTION

Norm R. Allen Jr.

H umanism is a rational, human-centered life stance that is primarily concerned with life in the here and now. This anthology is comprised of essays by *secular* humanists, i.e., agnostics or atheists. They discuss their reasons for rejecting theism and embracing a life-affirming nontheistic worldview.

Humanists often feel that they are alone, or that they are part of a misunderstood and despised minority. Many are afraid to come out of the closet due to fear of being ostracized, attacked, persecuted, or possibly killed by intolerant religionists.

With this in mind, African Americans for Humanism (AAH) was founded in 1989. AAH is a subdivision of the Council for Secular Humanism, headquartered near Buffalo, New York. It is primarily an educational organization that promotes humanist values such as crit-

9

ical thinking, humanist ethics, church/state separation, and an appreciation for scientific methods of investigation.

Rationality and secularism are not exclusively Western values. There are groups of secular humanists in Ghana, Nigeria, Senegal, Uganda, Kenya, Congo, and other African nations. Indeed, the Nigerian Humanist Movement, the Council for Secular Humanism, and AAH sponsored the first major international humanist conference to be held in sub-Saharan Africa in 2001.

Black humanist educators have left their mark on the world. Frank Arion is one of the leading authors in Curaçao, the Netherlands Antilles. He is the founder of the first humanist primary school in Curaçao, the Kolegio Erasmo (the Cap of Erasmus in Papiamento, Curaçao's native language). In response to the dogmatic and authoritarian Catholic community, Arion led the movement to establish the Fundashon Pa Skol Humanista na Papiamento (Foundation for Papiamento Humanist Schools) on December 1, 1986, Education Day in Curaçao. Later the group founded a strong movement to further humanist goals called Konsenshi Humanista (Humanist Conscience).

Despite strong opposition from Antillean conservatives, the school is successful. The curriculum focuses on science and technology. They have banned corporal punishment from the school, favoring positive reinforcement. The teachers are called "aunts" and "uncles," and the children love going to school. The humanist leaders in the movement hope to spread their teaching methods to all of the elementary schools in Curaçao.

In Nigeria the late Tai Solarin was a widely respected educator and human rights activist. Moreover, he was widely regarded as the only outspoken atheist in Nigeria. Solarin founded the Mayflower School in Ikenne, Ogun State. It is probably still the only secular high school in the nation. It produced Nigeria's first woman engineer and is one of the best schools in the country.

Solarin founded the school in response to the indoctrination forced upon African students in Catholic schools. At Mayflower there are secular messages on the school walls stressing the importance of education. Similarly, "Uncle Tai," as he was affectionately known, would wear a cap bearing the words "Knowledge is Light." The expression came from the great nineteenth-century freethinker and civil rights activist Robert Green Ingersoll, whom Solarin deeply admired.

Solarin had gone to prison many times for opposing military regimes in his country. He struggled for human rights to the very end. Indeed, he died the morning following his participation in a Walk for Justice in Lagos in opposition to the policies of then-Nigerian dictator Sani Abacha. He was eulogized in the *New York Times*, and Nigerians called him the "conscience of the nation." Humanist Nobel laureate Wole Soyinka dedicated his book *The Open Sore of a Continent* to Solarin.

Solarin's influence continues. Some of the African contributors to this volume were influenced and encouraged by his example. His memory was honored at the humanist conference in Nigeria. He was an independent thinker and a proud African. Like the contributors to this anthology, however, he scoffed at the suggestion that humanism is "un-African," or that religion must be placed at the center of Black life.

In an interview in the winter 1993/94 *Free Inquiry* magazine, Solarin responded to the first claim with the following statement:

> Humanism and atheism develop in the mind of man, not for a special breed of *Homo sapiens*, but for humanity, just as the wheel has been invented, not for whatever race invented it, but for humans everywhere. Whatever are branded "un-African," for the Aryan races are epithets for cheating. (p. 41)

Regarding the second claim, Solarin had this to say: "The blacks hold onto their God just as the drunken man holds on to the lamp post—for physical support only" (p. 40). Similarly, though many humanists believe that there are some positive aspects of religion, most believe that it is time to move forward by embracing a secular worldview.

Many Black religionists in particular are still attracted to a quietistic eschatology. Rather than seek rational solutions to the world's problems, they prefer to wait for the apocalypse and the divine rapture. In reality, however, they have been victimized by one failed prophecy after another. The Jehovah's Witnesses had predicted that the world would end during World War I, by 1975, and by the year 2000. Members of the Nation of Islam have been predicting "the coming destruction of America" since the early 1930s. Minister Louis Farrakhan predicted that Armageddon had begun prior to the Persian Gulf war between Iraq and Kuwait. The World Wide Church of God had predicted that the world would end in 1975, and again in 2000.

Shortly before 2000, religious Y2K enthusiasts all over the world had predicted gloom and doom. The year 2000 was undoubtedly the year in which Christ would return and/or the Apocalypse would take place. Religious authors Tim LaHaye and Jerry Jenkins sold ten million copies of their book on the Apocalypse, *Left Behind*. Jerry Falwell, Farrakhan, and other influential leaders made the failed prediction. As the year approached, however, some fatalists revised their dates or denied having made the predictions.

Other religionists predicted that the world would end late in the year 2000. Some asserted that the world would end in 2001. There are doomsday prophets pointing to the year 2007, and some claiming that 2030 will be the fateful year.

Fundamentalist Christians have been playing silly mind games with themselves and terrorizing their fellow human beings by making gloomy predictions for two thousand years. Humanists, however, maintain that enough is enough. Rather than nervously anticipating—and in some cases foolishly hoping for—the end of the world, human beings should be planning for a glorious future shaped by humanist ideals.

Contributors to this volume are hardly the stereotypical bitter atheists. They have not lost hope after abandoning theism. In many cases, they have developed a deeper appreciation for life in this world. Rather than simply searching for the meaning of life or having religionists force it upon them, these humanists have chosen to give their lives meaning. Some are highly critical of religion, and some are not. Some of them have had difficulty going it alone, and are still in search of a like-minded community. None of them, however, regards life as cold and empty.

There have been numerous anthologies by and about Black religionists. For example, in 1993 Steven Barboza wrote a book titled *American Jihad: Islam After Malcolm X*. The author discussed the lives and experiences of Muslims in the United States after Islam had become popularized by the Nation of Islam. In 1994 Jessie L. Embry wrote *Black Saints in a White Church: Contemporary African American Mormons,* in which she drew upon interviews with Black Mormons.

The Black Humanist Experience allows Black humanists to express their thoughts about humanism and their hope for the future. An evolved theory of humanism in which the relationship of the individual to society is discussed has yet to be written by a Black humanist. That project will be tackled at a later date. This volume, however, will provide justifications for a humanist life stance and give readers the opportunity to understand why secular humanists find nontheism to be such a tenable and respectable position.

1.

MILLENNIAL APOCALYPSE
A Street Preacher's View

Franz Vanderpuye

Several aspects of the new millennium, particularly its much-feared impact on the operation of computers worldwide, have been commented upon at length in various media. Little attention has been paid to a favorite hobbyhorse of millenarians elsewhere—that the end of the present millennium will trigger the final apocalyptic battle, marking the end of time following the defeat of the forces of evil represented by Satan, alias the Beast, and the fall of Babylon the Great and the entire worldly order.

Across the world quaint little sects and movements wait in anxious expectation of the binding of the Dragon, the final fulfillment of prophecy, and much else besides. There is no particular indication that our religions put such a literal interpretation on biblical prophecy; if they do, there appears to be precious little evidence here of preparation toward Armageddon. Or so I thought until I came across two gentlemen engaged in a heated argument on a scorching afternoon. Their grand religious dispute, as they saw it, centered on the meaning of the millennium and the unfolding of final events on this planet.

The first gentleman, his face framed by a gray, almost apostolic beard, spoke with an air of strained intellectuality. In an inimitable foreign accent, he supported his every assertion with a passage from a well-thumbed Bible which he kept tucked under his armpit. Off the top of his head he spun gripping tales of man's turpitude and iniquities. As the crowd followed each story, he quoted extensively from Daniel and Revelation, as well as from the Koran.

His opponent, a pugnacious little terrier of a man, was a study in skepticism. He favored a more allegorical interpretation of Scripture, and he countered that the other man's interpretations had captivated the imagination of cranks and quacks of all ages and generations down to the present. Millennium or no millennium, life goes on. He shook a bright tambourine to emphasize his points.

For some strange reason, the other man kept crates of bottled water by his side stressing, between bursts of speech, the Edenic properties of water as the source of all cleanliness. He would occasionally thunder that although his listeners' sins be as scarlet they would become as white as snow if they purchased a bottle of his "holy water."

The two had attracted an eager little crowd to their heated exchanges. The man with the accent continued his apocalyptic theme with a most determined attack upon all types of worldly pollution and immorality, every now and again directing a well-aimed remark at the skeptic. The heart of the unbeliever, he said, is like a sewer corrupting his entire being; and each sinner in our midst is like the rotten fruit which contaminates the entire bunch. Nothing short of sharp religious surgery is needed to restore the bad fruit to health. But when generation after generation, age after age, and century after century, irreligion, immorality, and social putrefaction continually overcome righteousness, the millennium must break like a bright cleansing morning to sweep all of diseased humanity's corruption away. After one thousand years of waiting, the millennium will unleash a series of events in fulfillment of ancient prophecy. Man's natural goodness will be restored only after the final judgment, when the undeserving will be processed through the white heat of hell's furnace.

The bearded speaker then painted a vivid picture of the roaring fires of hell. He painted in even starker colors the suffering of the condemned: a million hungry flames leaping around tortured, writhing bodies in a foul and dark place rent by the mighty cry of collective agony; a suffering Babel where numberless voices, trapped in the intensity of unquenchable fire and the infinite endlessness of eternity, combined to produce a strident, discordant, and most piteous noise; yet the complaint and sins of each voice remained distinct.

Undying worms gnawed at the innards of the condemned. The intense fear and horror of the place were multiplied a millionfold by indescribably grotesque creatures which lurked in ambush in the darkest corners, letting forth the most blood-curdling roars.

The arguing men of religion took turns mounting a small box near the gutter, and addressed the audience directly. The bearded man would peer myopically through gold-rimmed glasses, and with apocalyptic prediction, paint a most vivid picture of hell; a Dantean vision where, at the bottom of hell, a three-mouthed Lucifer feeds voraciously on traitors and sinners irredeemably entangled in earthly vice. He saw the devil's hoofprints in every evil-doer's deed, and attributed the individual failings of man to the mischief of two-horned demons. His persuasive tongue told of writhing pain and torturous punishment, but most essentially it dwelt on the coming apocalypse.

"As a man soweth so shall he reap," the preacher with the foreign accent said. "It matters little whether our sins are great or small; there is a price to pay for everything, especially when the last spark of life fails. There is nothing like a free meal." The end of every millennium, he declared, was a time of settlement of all human issues in the previous thousand years. We cannot escape the final judgment. Salvation does not grow on bushes. It is achieved through the relentless pursuit of righteousness. At the end of time the unrighteous cannot expect to get into the same boat as the righteous. The wicked and the innocent belong naturally to different boats.

On the other side of the street a noisy group of young men was gathered around white tables. Beside them were little stools packed with sizzling kabobs and glasses of beer with frothy white heads. They seemed attracted to the proceedings across the street, wondering who had brought such a worrisome hornet's nest about their ears. They cocked their heads to catch the words of the disputants. Initially they reacted with apathy, but soon they were drawn into active participation. They broke into a brief little argument of their own, but presently agreed that the two gentlemen were fretting themselves over a matter that is best left to individual judgment. One coolly commented that no such nonsense had ever before been imagined by *Homo sapiens* as the idea, obviously held by these theists, that the holder of an opinion should attempt by vociferous means to impose his personal beliefs on others through public quarrels.

I had had enough food for thought for one day. Back home, I started reflecting on my personal beliefs vis-à-vis my immediate environment. My encounter with those two religious protagonists taught me two lessons: First, how sad it must be to believe in a god of blood and ruthlessness; second, how important it is to have the courage to dissent from it.

The very life of an African is defined by religion. This was very well captured by Emmanuel Kofi Mensah (Ghanaian founder of Action for Humanism in Nigeria) when he wrote that from the cradle to the grave, "the African's relationship to the family, clan, tribe, and everything that sustains—or weakens—the African life, has its taproot embedded deeply in the soil of religion. This includes law, war, peace, politics, economics, celebrations, and so forth."[1] The conception of a child in Africa is considered to be a gift from God (or the gods). Naming ceremonies after the birth of the child therefore go through various forms of religious rituals depending on the ethnic group or clan. Therefore by default, a child is born into a religion, and his or her whole life is shaped by such beliefs and practices.

It is, therefore, generally inconceivable to challenge any form of religion in Africa, be it traditional African religion (animism), Christianity, Islam, or those Asian religions which are currently making inroads in the continent.

I was born into a middle-class Christian family, although my paternal grandfather had an aristocratic background, having been trained as a Minister of the Word and a lawyer (he later became the first African attorney of the Accra Traditional Council in the colonial administration). His father (my great-grandfather) founded the Walton Church (Wesley) in Accra. With such a solid Christian background, it came as no surprise that I was baptized into the Presbyterian faith on the eighth day after my birth (my grandmother is a staunch Presbyterian). At the age of nineteen years, I had to undergo the confirmation ceremony like any other Ghanaian high-school graduate. But that was just when my broadened scope on life led me to start questioning the deliberate attempt by society to divert people from the path of natural development of consciousness and individuality to insistence on regimented belief in divine justification for human laws. The issue of superior authority of faith, as opposed to reason, started bothering me, and I decided to exploit the leeway offered by acts of natural teenage rebellion to explore the world beyond religion.

The real breakthrough for me in severing my relations with religion came when I entered college to study journalism and mass communication. The course content required studies in logic and introduction to philosophy, and these two disciplines gave me a better understanding of the diversity of ideas and some of the reasons underlying them. I had begun to appreciate the devastating effect of blind superstition on the social, cultural, and economic life of Ghanaians and, for that matter, all Africans.

Religion is based on fear of the unknown, and this can be found in the underlying doctrines guiding all religious persuasions. But the most damaging effect of this fear of the unknown can be found in Africa, where the crippling effect is manifested in a general inferiority complex and mental slavery that grips Africans, forcing people to fail in realizing their potential and thereby attributing all their failures in life to the designs and machinations of witchcraft or destiny. The fear of economic deprivation, fear of the mysterious, and especially fear of death serve as the foundation of religion in Africa.

If there is any doubt that man creates God in his own image, only to allow God to destroy him, then there is no better place to test that hypothesis than in Africa. Fear causes the African to become superstitious, to believe in an all-powerful God, to believe in ghosts, in witches, in palmistry, in horoscopy, in fact, in all the unknowables which have chained mankind to mental slavery for ages.

As I started becoming critical of dogmatism, I gradually weaned myself from the alleged power of prayer. I opted for a life guided by reason and freed from dogmas of God. I freed myself from the dictates of stifling traditional beliefs and suffocating Christian teachings. I found myself in the fold of humanism, which inspires me to achieve the highest level possible by using my mind rather than relying on an unseen benevolent hand.

As observed by Paul Edwards in his article "God and the Philosophers," the notion of God, according to Friedrich Nietzsche (1844–1900), is extremely harmful because it is employed, especially by Christian moralists, to denigrate earthly happiness and other secular values.[2] "The concept of God," he quotes Nietzsche, "was invented as the opposite of the concept of life—everything detrimental, poisonous and slanderous, and all deadly hostility to life, was bound together in one horrible unit."[3]

To theistic believers, human life has no meaning in a universe without God. And therein lies the conflict between irrational blind faith and rational, logical minds. The many myths, deceptions, and contradictions in the Bible have been examined by many other learned people. Suffice it to say that I believe that the world functions under natural laws—it has nothing to do with the actions or reactions of God. The men who wrote the Bible believed that the world had been created by a personal God, that when misfortune struck, it was due to God's displeasure, and when things went well, God was pleased with them. Vern Bullough, senior editor of *Free Inquiry*, writes, "Within the movement of reparative therapy in the fundamentalist Christian community, failures are never acknowledged. The pretense remains that all one needs to do to solve all life's difficulties is to be a believer."[4]

Rt. Rev. Desmond Tutu, South African former chairman of the World Council of Churches (and a former leading antiapartheid campaigner), is well known for his philosophical remark, "Faith is a risk I will never risk being without." Each time I saw footage of this statement on America's Cable News Network (CNN), I was reminded of my favorite cartoon in *Free Inquiry*. This cartoon shows a little boy going on a walk and being held by his mother. The two met an elderly woman sporting a T-shirt with the inscription "*I am with Him.*" Apparently puzzled because the elderly woman was walking alone, our little friend asked, "Aren't you a little old to have an imaginary friend?"

To get rid of the widespread mass appeal of superstition in Africa, its peoples must be given the opportunity for education, particularly secular education. For us in Africa, this is a tall order, given the fact that state and religion control every facet of social and economic life. Policy makers are themselves religious, and their personal idiosyncrasies shape the everyday life of their fellow citizens. This calls for preventing churches from controlling educational institutions (there are quite a number under their direct control in Ghana), and making education more secular. Secular humanists should be more involved in this fight against religious domination. Unfortunately, few people in this part of the world can be counted as skeptics, and even fewer people have the courage to stand up and fight for secularization of our societies.

I have come to the conclusion that prayer is one of the manipulative methodologies underlying religion and cannot be factored into solving any real problem. I don't believe in prayers, I believe in hard work.

Why did I abandon my religious beliefs? In his book *Farewell to God: My Reasons for Rejecting the Christian Faith*, Charles Templeton answered the same question thus: "Should one continue to base one's life on a system of belief that—for all its occasional wisdom and frequent beauty—is demonstrably untrue?"[5] I rest my case.

For those who continue to interpret biblical prophecy literally and to long for an afterlife in which their unfulfilled hopes and dreams can finally be met, they had better listen to an Akan[6] saying, *baabiara ni ha*. Loosely, this means "Heaven's here on earth."

NOTES

1. Emmanuel Kofi Mensah, "The African Case," *AAH Examiner* 9, no. 2 (summer 1999).

2. Paul Edwards, "God and the Philosophers," *Free Inquiry* 19, no. 1 (winter 1998/99).

3. Ibid.

4. Ibid.

5. Charles Edwards, *Farewell to God: My Reasons for Rejecting the Christian Faith* (Toronto: McClelland & Stewart, 1996).

6. The largest ethnic group in Ghana.

2.

HUMANISM, REASON, AND EMOTION

Leonard Harris

I arrived at a humanist position—the position that all persons had something in common to which they were entitled and that what they had in common could not be explained by reference to religious texts—at an early age. I remember reading the Bible as a teenager and wondering how all the wonderful stories could actually be true. I also wondered what would happen to people who never read those stories—were they eternally condemned to a lower ranking in the afterlife simply because they could not read? I wondered how life could be explained by these stories.

I never really questioned whether others were human. The idea that people could not be human or were either inherently inferior or superior was not a view I encountered until one year into college, and then the source was the Ku Klux Klan. I hitchhiked from Columbus,

Ohio, to Wilberforce, Ohio, in a pickup truck in which a White driver gave me a ride. We went through a small town with telephone poles shaped like crosses in which people were preparing a Klan rally. The driver said that the town was preparing as if it was just another small-town festival. This was my first encounter with evil. Although the concept of evil has religious overtones, I know of no other term that captures the depth of what it is to have a banality toward the misery of others, to glow in the pain of others, and to do so without remorse or rethinking. It is not only that evil is reveling in the pain of others for no reason, but the "no reason" is that the other is not counted.

The second time I encountered the concept of unequal persons was when I discovered the Nation of Islam. The Nation did not believe that Whites were inherently inferior—at least as far as I could tell—but rather that Whites were inherently different and evil.

The Klan and the Nation seemed so fanatically and obviously wrong that I never veered from my belief in the oneness of humanity. Not even when, in 1963, Glenville High School students in Cleveland, Ohio—of which I was one student—marched to the White high school because they had trapped the few Blacks that attended inside, and we went to free them. The students taunted us, threw rocks, and the police protected Whites while trying to arrest us. I never thought of the Whites as either inferior, inherently different, or invariably evil. It was the Klan that introduced real evil. And it is the commonness of humanity—that fact that we are fundamentally emotive beings constituted in similar ways but capable of a vast range of emotions—that makes the possibility of evil a horror that could be practiced by any individual or group.

My family was Baptist. We attended Shiloh Baptist Church at Fifty-fifth and Scoville Avenue; across the street from the projects (apartments designed for the least well off). My grandparents, Warren and Millie Chappell, were not only members, but helped found the church in 1916. This was unknown to me at the time; I knew, however, that my whole family—uncles, aunts, and cousins—were members. Shiloh was a grand church in those days. It had a magnificent domed ceiling, baptismal pool just behind the pulpit, seats for all of the deacons behind the pulpit, and a choir section to the left. The paint is now tattered and it just looks like a small church, but growing up, it was magnificent. It made me feel that I was in a house of the holy when I entered, just because it was so grand.

I never voiced my doubts about the truth of Christianity while I was at home. Never. The closest I ever came was when I told my parents that I was going to be a conscientious objector in 1966. Usually, conscientious objectors believed that military life was against their religious beliefs. However, I claimed that I had moral reasons for refusing to join the army, and therefore it was against my basic conscience. I was not going to be drafted into the army and possibly be sent to fight in Vietnam. I had no intentions of joining the army or fighting so that White folk could gain profit from the sale of weapons. My parents did not want me in the army, but they were not comfortable with my claim that I was a conscientious objector. They were not sure if I would get in trouble. My father never trusted thieving ministers. My mother and aunts were faithful. "Conscientious objector" was in no one's vocabulary. The subject of religion was never broached. Undergraduate college students, as it turned out, were not eligible for the draft.

I think, in hindsight, that my aunts and uncles cast an aura over my sense of the mysterious and my respect for persons of faith. My church-going aunts were everywhere. Aunt Mary lived on the corner of my street, Forest Grove, and aunts Mildred Martin and Evelyn Thomas lived a few streets away. My uncle Isaac Chappell lived on the next street and my uncle Warren Chappell lived not far away. I could never fathom the idea of debating religious views with my aunts, let alone my uncles. But when my father and mother drove me to Central State University, Wilberforce, Ohio, in 1966 in my family's white Pontiac and I saw the "Central State University" sign in front of the campus, I knew. I knew that I would never return to Cleveland to live. I still recall how the sign looked from the back seat.

College provided me a social space to talk about ideas without feeling as if expressing ideas would invariably hurt people I loved. That sort of freedom is impossible to describe. It also provided a community of persons motivated to try to improve human life. Radicals, for example, whether Black nationalist, socialist, or communist, all shared a deep emotional inclination to risk their lives to improve the lives of future generations.

My humanist sensibilities now suggest the following: We should just give up. We have fought a gallant battle. We have fought against pagans, Muslims, Christians, Buddhists, Hindus, and every manner of religionist. It is not just that atheists, agnostics, and freethinkers cannot win against religionists. (I am, admittedly, a freethinker and a bit of a spiritualist—finding most comforts around the Buddhist and B'hai—but not a believer. Possibly, I feel more comfortable with persons with these faith commitments because they are far less racist than Christian, and less doctrinaire than Muslims or Hindus.)

Religionists favor a particular faith that they believe should be institutionalized, codified, and perpetuated. In addition, religionists are necessarily foundationalist. That is, they must believe that there are some definitive truths and definitive methods of thought about the ultimate nature of the universe, God, and what all sentient beings should believe for all time. Religionists believe that pragmatism, utilitarianism, instrumentalism, rationalism, behaviorism, dialectics, and all other epistemologies are only tools of thought. There is a truth that is to some degree mysterious and inaccessible to tools of thought for religionists. That truth requires faith and a sense of accepting that that truth is absolute. The form of the absolute truth might be belief in an omnipresent and omnipotent God, nothingness (that which nothing can be said), or the multiple presences of godheads or the God of and for a given people or city.

Religionists are all wrong. But their sense of connection to the universe, their sense of knowing what is foundationally true, their feeling of being a vessel of the holy and a knower of what is the case for all time is very appealing. So appealing that evolutionary explanations of life do not even mean that an evolutionist might not also be a religionist (an evolutionist, for example, can simply believe that evolution provides the best explanation of development, but the possibility of development and existence in general may rest with faith in a supernatural being or force). Materialist explanations, such as Marxist accounts, are often explanations that, after demolishing the idea that religionists are not independent ahistorical thinkers, replaced their explanations with a deep and abiding faith about the ability of a materialist to predict the future and a faith in workers to be more morally inclined than capitalists. In addition, hermeneutical, phenomenological, and existenialist accounts, for all of the contentions that humans are capable of individual choice, tell us to find meaning in a meaningless universe. However, philosophers from such traditions have never authored social movements that liberated any social group.

Almost no one risks their lives for their neighbor or sacrifices for their children guided by the belief that their sacrifices are meaningless to anyone but themselves. I am certain that there are virtually no absolute egoists on the planet. I am equally certain that sentient life cannot exist dominated by such egoists. It is in everyone's individual interest to steal and to never tell the truth unless it is reasonably predicted that some form of gain is to be acquired. Poor egoists are rare; everyone steals from them and they can never improve their lot without compassion and trust from others—traits that they cannot consistently receive unless they demonstrate such traits. And in a hedonistic world of egoists, only free riders would survive. But in a world full of hedonistic free riders, no one exists past a generation. That is to say, no one would be compelled to sacrifice for the next generation. This is so because no sense of collective responsibility would exist and there would be no sense of caring about one's future reputation, progeny, or loved ones. A good egoist need not care about such matters.

I want to give up the fight. Forget about destroying religionists by destroying the rational basis of their beliefs. Showing that religionists are irrational, hold internally incoherent or contradictory views, and are terrible predictors of the future has not proven effective—and it is not likely to prove effective.

Reason is a cheap substitute for faith. Pragmatic, utilitarian, or dialectical tools of reasoning are of no use when a sense of loss, emptiness, and finite existence creeps into our consciousness. Antireligionists have been too dependent on reasoning as a tool and far less reliant on the obvious: people, including antireligionists, are emotive agents.

Science fiction and religiosity seem to me to be often conjoined because they elicit similar emotions and rely on equally fantastic claims. In that vein, I offer the following short story to help account for the location of my current humanist sensibilities.

WHY SCIENCE FICTION SHOULD REPLACE RELIGIONS: OR WHAT HAPPENED WHEN THE ALIENS LANDED

Aliens have landed. (The first problem we have after the announcement of their landing is whether to describe them as aliens. Having arrived, they are no longer alien to the Earth.) In any event, it seems as if they have lived on Earth for eons. They are playing a movie on a huge screen mounted on top of Entoto Mountain, Addis Ababa, Ethiopia. The movie, if that is what it can be called, is a fast-running history of the Rift Valley. We see at the beginning a group of small apelike beings, fires, cooking, and some pretty gruesome rapes and murders, dances, hugs, markets, walking, in-the-bush deification, rites of passage such as praying, voting, and giving speeches, and a few scenes of X-rated sex. Different sorts of persons perform these acts over time. Each group is gradually replaced by a new group. The movie ends with tourists visiting the Rift Valley and then starts again. All vegetation and anyone living on or near Entoto Mountain died in one week. Why, exactly, is still a mystery. Possibly it was their sinful life, but more likely it had to do with unique microbes responsible for dysfunctions and abnormal levels of heat.

I am reporting from nearly ten miles away, behind military barricades, and from inside an office building with a clear view of the mountain. I am near Mexico Square in Addis Ababa and as far as I can tell, and this has been confirmed by military reconnaissance, the closer you get to the base of the mountain the hotter it gets. We, however, have a clear view of what the aliens look like. They look like corporeal dark shadows. Movements of irradiant shades; they seem light in weight, almost feathery, and only appear outside of a gigantic hole in the side of Entoto Mountain briefly, and then, back in.

All explanations are suspended. All conceptions of a human teleology of our own making, all conceptions of a human teleology created because of our desire to be free from unnecessary exploitation, all conceptions of a human teleology created by supernatural powers presaged in ancient religious texts are obviously empty.

We are left naked, with only our commonness, memories of aunts and uncles, and the need to have faith in at least the possibility of a future for our progeny.

3.

MY JOURNEY FROM CATHOLICISM TO HUMANISM

Carolyn M. Dejoie

My journey from Catholicism to humanism has been convoluted and involved. I have sampled many areas of endeavor searching for a belief system which coincided with my quest for fulfillment, and also for a group steadfast in its commitment to be rooted in a philosophy of ethical approaches to life.

Humanism, for me, reaches beyond the question of deity. It is an ideology that incorporates values and principles which create the infrastructure for ethical conduct. The group for which I still search is one of open minds concerned with critical inquiry and social interests. This community should be one in which the members can be embraced in fellowship and a sense of belonging within a cooperative environment of shared values and vision. Too, the members should be willing to involve themselves individually in introspection regarding the ethical quality of their lives. This personal inventory, analysis of values, and its application to life situations will demonstrate its effectiveness in regard to ethical conduct.

The focus of this group would be self-government reinforced by one's own self-designed values and ethical judgment to foster personal growth and life enrichment of one's self and of others.

No dogma or creed would be included in the purpose or mission of this group. Rational thought and a healthy respect for scientific evidence would be integral components of the organization.

As I recall, I had questions regarding Catholicism very early in reference to original sin. I resented being punished immediately at birth and permanently for the sins of Adam and Eve. Earning a living "by the sweat of the brow," struggling to survive, enduring painful labor in childbirth, and finally dying were elements of the punishment for the inherited "sin."

My mother revered nuns and priests. This was her upbringing. She and her two sisters attended boarding school, as was customary for French and Creole families. This was a Catholic school—Holy Rosary, in Lafayette, Louisiana—under the auspices of the nuns of the Holy Family. We lived in New Orleans and were born and bred Catholics. However, in spite of my religious heritage, my position as a young adult was that the clergy and related personnel chose their professions and I had chosen mine. I contended that they did not merit sanctimonious consideration from me or anyone for their choices, that they could be differed with, and that I and others had a right to challenge their authoritarian pronouncements.

There were other areas in which I differed with religious practices and questions for which I searched for answers. As a very young woman, I deemed that funerals were not justified. They were expensive, sad, and a product for the living, not the dead. I held the belief that cemeteries utilized much land that could be put to better purposes in order to enrich the lives of the living.

As a child I was expected to go to confession on a regular basis— intervals not longer than two weeks. Not having anything to confess I would just say that I missed saying morning or night prayers or other simplistic omissions or actions like answering my mother back.

On one occasion, as a young child, not knowing what to confess, I told the priest, not knowing what the word meant, that I had committed adultery. At best, reporting one's most personal frailties and faults to an unseen man hidden in a cubicle is mysterious and puts the confessor in an unfair position. Too, characterizing the priest—a mere man—as a representative of God was more than I could accept.

As far as Communion, as a matter of course, I express to my fundamentalist and Bible-thumping acquaintances that Communion is no less than cannibalism, if one believes that he or she is consuming the body and blood of anyone.

Later in life my perspective of negating "sin" was shocking to those believers, who were awestruck at such blasphemy. This, for them, was contrary to the teachings of the Bible. I believe "sin" is a religious term, perhaps in lay language consistent with evil, wicked, mean, anti-social behavior and other terms with similar meaning, except with an added caveat, "offensive to God." "Sin" and consequential punishment are man's concoction for social control.

I lived many years in Mexico City but visited the United States regularly. I had always had questions about the Catholic practice of fasting and abstaining from eating meat on Fridays. I was told that this sacrifice was in recognition of the Crucifixion. The falsity of this concept was evident because this practice did not extend to Mexico, a deeply Catholic country. The explanation was that Mexico was a poor country and the inhabitants had to eat whatever was available. So as soon as we crossed the United States-Mexican border the rules changed.

My son made his first Communion in Mexico and enjoyed the ornate candles, refreshments, and festive celebration. The purpose, for us, was not so much religious as to be participants in the sociocultural customs of the area.

Moving back to the United States, I began searching for a community in which I felt comfortable but not compelled to practice rituals or participate in mythology-based activities. I sampled Unity, with which I was somewhat familiar due to a close friend who had provided me with related material years earlier. A woman minister headed this particular church. However, that too was unfulfilling. I avoided Protestant churches as I had never had any affiliation with Protestantism. I was taught that Protestant churches were not of God but man-made churches—that the Catholic church was the only true church.

I was also totally repelled by the preaching, the hell and brimstone, fornication, and other themes of television evangelists I had chanced upon. Moreover, they were loud, boisterous, and uncivilized in contrast to the sedate, organized, and universal structure of Catholicism. And the uncontrolled behavior of the congregants was appalling and frightening—fainting, talking in tongues, and other conduct that necessitated white-clad "aides" to calm them.

Not finding a group—a community—that offered social and emotional support without the religiosity, I avoided churches, temples, and other places of worship. This word *worship*, too, is unacceptable to me. It is humbling and without merit. Prayer conjures an image of begging. In fact, all of the language, ceremonies, and rituals are repelling.

My last, but fulfilling, involvement with a like group (until my departure) was as a member of a lay-led Unitarian Universalist Society. It was not designated a church, but a fellowship. I enjoyed the multi-disciplined speakers and themes, the focus on social concerns, and the structure. Members directed the Sunday meetings. The building was called the meeting house. The financial contributions were discretionary, and the activities also included those of a social nature which fostered a cohesive community (circle dinners, that is, small groups members hosted at their homes or ethnic restaurants, and other enjoyable events).

Alas, I was painfully wounded by my abrupt personal discovery that this caring religious congregation had no semblance of caring or religion in its most extended interpretation. Having experienced an abusive encounter with a member known for her erratic behavior, I appealed to the board for remedy, which was encouraged by the regional director of the Unitarian Universalist Churches to whom I went for support. Disregarding the views of the regional director and my justified pleas, no remedy or reprimand was granted. Callous behavior extended to the whole congregation as not one person made inquiry of me or offered comfort or concern.

I was convinced that I had seriously misjudged the group, or more accurately stated, that the integrity, principles, and values had not thoroughly been tested until then. However, I felt that I could no longer associate with persons whom I judged to be character-deficient.

Religions do little, if anything, to direct the congregants on a more viable path to positive human productivity, creativity, and humanistic conduct. The total concept of faith, prayer, and God's will limits the probability of personal action. Whereas excessive energy is expended in services to the church, the minister, and church activities which are deity-based, I choose to make contributions to individuals following my personal humanistic principles and values, to assist them in enriching and enhancing their lives.

I then invested my interest, energy, and passion in forming a secular humanist group. As the lives of groups attest, there is great interest in the beginning, after which losing members is not uncommon. This—coupled with one lively dissenter who single-handedly used all of his forces to sabotage my efforts—depleted my energy. His sole interest was "God-bashing" and separation of church and state, picketing, and other demonstrations. Our purpose and mission were far broader than his views.

The fatal blow to the Secular Humanists of Madison, Wisconsin, was the resignation of the Director of Community Programs from the Council for Secular Humanism.

As a young adult, in times of stress I prayed to various saints, made novenas, and engaged in Catholic rituals to resolve my concerns. When my son was very ill, he and I journeyed to Lourdes to be dipped in the miracle waters. That was one of the most moving and gratifying experiences of my life. It was a quasi-transformation. I was calm, contemplative, and at peace. For a long time I could only sit in the warm rays of the sun. These events did not deter me from the deep-seated incredulity imbedded in religious teachings. Whereas I had serious doubts about standard religions, I had nothing to replace Catholicism.

As I had done earlier—having been exposed to logic and college courses that provoked rational thinking, books, articles, and other published material which invoked inquiries on my part—I gradually began examining traditional teachings and reconstructing my belief system. Rational thinking and scientific evidence did not permit me to accept the virgin birth and other "documented" events in the Bible. I also realized that religious history does not coincide with world history, cultural and social history, and science.

Though I do not envision a "God" personified in the likeness of a human being, and I am completely committed to science and evidence, I am not at odds with perhaps a force yet undiscovered by science (a magnetic force, perhaps, that influences events), thought waves, or other phenomena yet unheard of. In this sense I am a trans-humanist who considers that we are in the process of evolving.

For me, humanism does not include vile condemnation, ridicule, and sarcastic statements against a deity. For me, humanism is founded on principles, value systems, and rational thought that lay a foundation for ethical conduct. It is a belief that one can function humanistically without an authority figure—a deity—monitoring, judging, rewarding, or punishing us. We can chart our own course of behavior imbued in our character, integrity, and dignity.

At this point I identify myself as a humanist, but I am extremely lonely and isolated in my belief system. I have no community with whom to discuss issues, concepts, current happenings, or individuals, or who can support and contribute to my position. I continue to search and perhaps within another denomination I would be able to form a discussion group on humanism. However, this would be less than fulfilling, as the group would be a subdivision of the church and under its auspices. Being a part of a larger or national humanist society for expansive contact, information, and participation would not be possible. It is most difficult emotionally and psychologically to answer the question, "Where do I go from here?"

4.

LIVING ON THE THRESHOLD OF MAGNIFICENCE
An Autobiographical Essay

Ranjini L. Thaver

I was born in apartheid South Africa, one of eight children of poor and uneducated parents. My father, a depressed alcoholic, was physically and emotionally abusive. My mother, who took charge of our economic welfare, was an amazing source of strength to her children, even as she suffered under the brutality of my father. Being poor and Black, we lived under the atrocity of a class system compounded exponentially by the intransigent racist system of apartheid. Trying to survive under such a system left no time to experience love. Feeling an everlasting hollowness, helplessness, hopelessness, and lovelessness, I sought suicide as my sanctuary at the age of nine. When my suicide attempt failed, I decided there was a reason for me to live, and even though I continued to invite death to my door, I no longer attempted to take my own life.

At the ripe age of twelve years, I was charmed into the conviction that Jesus was God. The magic lay in the evangelist's exhortation that Jesus loved me, cherished me, and would fill all the emptiness in my heart. Having found my solution, I embarked upon strategies to ensure that God chose me as one of the select few who was worthy of the limited space in heaven. I converted into a devout Christian disciple, attending church regularly, taking catechism classes, and teaching Sunday school. I even developed the art of speaking in tongues,[1] a mark of a truly special person in Jesus' sight, according to my pastor.

Since I had once literally felt like "a filthy rag" I became convinced that it was only the dying love of Christ that saved me. As a filthy rag, I attributed all good that life offered me to Jesus' doing, and I wanted everyone else to see that no greater love could be experienced than that which came from Him. Filled with great inspiration, I became a missionary, preaching "high on the mountaintops" that Christ was God without whom we were lost and empty.

My first experience with questioning Christianity's nobility came a few months after my conversion. My pastor repeatedly warned that non-Christians would burn in hell if they did not find salvation in Jesus Christ. When I asked him one day about the fate of children who could not become Christian because of their parents, he replied that anyone under twelve years would be exempt from hell as they were too young to make their own decisions. In my simplistic but humane mind, I began praying profusely that the world would come to an end so that fewer children could reach the age of twelve, thereby escaping eternal death.

As the years progressed, I increasingly questioned Christianity but still continued as a passionate Christian. In college I became exposed to different theories of life and living. Carl Rogers's proposal that only unconditional love is true love was my first major breaking point with Christianity. I awakened one day to declare to Jesus and the world that I was not a filthy rag, but a wonderful human being, worthy of receiving and offering unconditional love, rather than the conditional love advocated by the Bible. In my newfound love for self and the world, I began to see the relationship between all forms of oppression and Christianity.

Just as Christianity decreed that those who did not serve Christ totally and unquestionably as "fishers of men" would fall short of the glory of God and meet eternal hell, the sole reason for the existence of Black people was to serve the needs of the White race. Those who defied this law were to be flogged for being lazy good-for-nothing niggers such as America's Kunta Kinte and South Africa's Steve Biko. I began seeing why apartheid reigned so powerfully for more than a century and I comprehended the long-term success of slavery. As Whites tried to appease God by leading good Christian lives (as articulated by racist missionaries and scholars) and falling prostrate at Jesus' feet, Blacks who were subjugated to Whites through political, economic, religious, and social forces tried to appease them by being good house-slaves and servants. White and Black people, conditioned by social, economic, political, and religious forces, reinforced the vicious cycle of oppression. Those who cried out against these forms of oppression were burned at the stakes as violators of the rule of law.

In my liberation I also developed an awareness of how the Bible reinforced the subordination of women to men. This notion was embodied in my mother who, though my father dehumanized her, was placated by the belief that this was her test on Earth for eternal peace in heaven. Equally ominous, and embodied in my father, came the wisdom that men in abiding by the biblical image of being a master of one's household were duty-bound to control their household through the fear of God. In order to secure their own happiness in life after death, men were compelled to subordinate women to their providence, and women were equally compelled to obey their husbands.

The Bible's command to accept suffering on Earth for gains in heaven also found its manifestation in the appeasement of the poor and oppressed people of this world. The poor were blessed and had to wait to "inherit the earth." Those with "talents" had to ensure they multiplied them or else they would lose them, resulting in the form of rugged capitalism that we see today. Politically oppressed people were commanded to respect their governments that were supposedly ordained by God, thereby perpetuating the oppression of one group of people by another.

In exploring other religions I learned that at the most superficial layer, these religions all reinforced passivity to oppression, sexism, heterosexuality, and prejudice of one sort or another. I understood there were a few people who managed to triumph over the written word to understand the spirit of an action-reflection-oriented life, such as Gandhi, Mandela, Martin Luther King Jr., Malcolm X, and Mother Teresa, among others. But for the rest of society, religion served as the opium of the people. To continue to belong to a religion, for me, implied serving opium to most people. Liberation from all forms of religion became vital to the process of breaking away from a fragmented consciousness for my human dignity. In developing my own philosophy of life I found people such as Carl Rogers, Abraham Maslow, Paula Freire, and Angela Davis, among others, appealing. Now as I stride away from fragmented living toward a more integrated humanist life, I understand the examples of people such as Jesus, Muhammad, Vishnu, Brahma, and Buddha among wise figures. Contemporaneously Einstein, Angela Davis, Malcolm X, Gandhi, Mother Teresa, Mandela, and others have served as my inspiration that to be human is to live a life in praxis. I have learned to love myself enormously, and in so doing, have developed a great love for all of life. I have learned to also see the virtue of those who need to believe in outside forces for their sense of self and dignity—after all, it was this element that facilitated my own transformation. At the same time, I am able to enjoy those humans, embodied in my sons, who in receiving nearly unconditional love as children do not rely on supernatural forces for their own sense of self-worth.

It is with my experience in mind that I would like to articulate a credo on being humanist:

- To be humanist is to derive delight in knowing that my relationship with the universe is within the parameters of my own consciousness. My consciousness, with increasing discernment, can expand beyond the boundaries limited by conditioned relationships with the world around me.
- To be humanist is to accept that the human experience is a dualistic one with tendencies to be violent and unjust on the one hand, and on the other hand to be compassionate, trusting, and altruistic.

- To be humanist is to be action-oriented while maintaining a seriousness to deep reflections about our actions; to transcend the vicious cycle of oppression by serving neither as an oppressor nor as the oppressed.
- To be a humanist teacher is to continuously engage self and students in the meaning of life through our subject matter. Our role is to encourage our students to question all that they are exposed to, and to see that education at the most apparent level reinforces conditioned lives. But as with all other social forms, the task is for the student to transcend the obvious.
- Finally, to be humanist is to be physically, mentally, and emotionally harmonious with life—to love deeply all that exists. It is to live on the threshold of magnificence!

NOTE

1. I listened carefully to all the other tongue-speakers and then synthesized the various tongues into my unique concoction.

5.

A BELIEVER'S TESTIMONY

Igwe Ucheakolam

One fateful day while I was coming from an evening lecture during my years in the university, a thought occurred to me that perhaps God does not exist. This was a very sudden and seemingly unacceptable thought for a teacher's son from a conservative Catholic family.

I had tried unsuccessfully to suppress this question for many years, and at a point during my secondary school days, I even stopped going to church. What a strange thing to do in a community where going to mass on Sundays was like competing for a trophy, and being an altar boy was an exalted aspiration. My father was a dedicated Roman Catholic, and my eldest brother was a would-be Catholic priest. My lackadaisical attitude toward religion constituted some sort of embarrassment to them, and to the whole family. When I got to the university, the situation changed dramatically when I was caught by the Pentecostal fire. I remember vividly how my sister stage-managed my conversion by initially handing me over to a "spiritual big brother" in school. It was like being a born-again Christian, the only viable option for me. I had to yield to a lot of preaching, pressure, and subtle threats. I got to know a lot of songs, and I memorized scriptural verses. I was admitted into the cult of spirituality, with many sanctimonious brothers and holy sisters always around me.

One of the most outstanding events of my stint with Pentecostalism was the Holy Ghost baptism. It took place at a meeting somewhere in the town. On that day things went on as usual, until the officiating minister announced "God's intention to baptize some people." He gave us a chance to stand on our feet. I was the third person to do so—out of sheer curiosity. Immediately, one fat woman came toward me and started praying for me. She held my head hard and tilted it backward, and then spoke directly to my face. I waited one to six minutes, but she didn't leave me. Suddenly, she rolled out a strange language: "Reman Santara . . . shekindaraba. . . ." At the point when I couldn't endure the pain, I started twisting my mouth and murmuring something. When she saw this, she suddenly pushed me down. "I had fallen on anointing." Subsequently, it was all tongues on the streets and in the lecture room. Even during midnight, I murmured what she taught me, and added my own of course. A lot of people on campus began associating me with deep spirituality. At this point, it seemed rather incomprehensible to allow the question of God's existence to come up again. I attributed this to wandering thoughts from the devil, and quickly called upon the blood of Jesus, sealing it up with a syllable of glossolalia.

This was my second year in school, and my born-again sister in the United States was occasionally sending me a few dollars for my schooling, and indirectly monitoring my growth in the Lord. All her letters to me often bore that uninteresting cliché: "How is Jesus?" as if I had to answer this question in order to be on her payroll. I never did!

As I was approaching my hostel one day, I began to imagine how my sister would feel if I jettisoned Christianity and God. She would automatically stop sending me money, and that would mark the end of my education. What about my fellow brethren on campus? They would ostracize me and my social life would collapse. Even as these disquieting and frightening consequences stared at me, I calmly pressed on in my search for the truth. I managed to get back to the church, though I never stopped questioning several anomalies and pretensions that went on in the name of God. I queried why somebody would wear tattered clothes, go without earrings, or cease using perfumes and deodorants in the name of piety. I became critical of arranged marriages for couples without courtship, medical reports, and the like, based on the whims and caprices of one inexperienced pastor or of a parochial and ignorant marriage committee.

One thing was crystal clear, I was falling for reason, my faith was depreciating, my dogmatism degenerating, and my "godliness" fast eluding me. I continued to grow in my disgust for all superstitions and spurious claims which cannot stand the test of scientific scrutiny.

Now I have graduated from the university, from what people might say, and from what my sister could do. I can no longer disguise my disgust for religious hypocrisy, lies, deceit, and superstition. I find no reason to fear or believe in God or gods. I rise up to my daily tasks courageously and confidently with neither the guilt of sin nor the fear of either a devil or a supernatural deity. I do not long for eternal bliss—a spiritual illusion. I consult no seer or pastor. I have embraced humanism as my guiding philosophy, as an enriching and worthwhile alternative to the sanctimonious and hypocritical life of dogmatism and religion, which has tormented my life hitherto. The human-centered life stance has ushered me into the realm of complete independence of mind and body. It has taken me into a regime of creative self-confidence, making me a captain—and no longer a captive—of life. I now know that my destiny depends on me, not on God or his human representatives.

Humanism can help humanity take its destiny in its hands and save our world from religious violence, ethnic genocide, holocaust, and other social ills and tragedies that have stained the course of human history and civilization. By emphasizing education as a potent and effective tool in the uplifting and development of individual potentials, humanism can be of enormous benefit, particularly in the developing world where ignorance and illiteracy have continued to frustrate and obstruct not only economic growth, but also general human development and progress.

The humanist philosophy can also help expose religious lies, falsehoods, and tricks which the "babalawos," imams, priests, and prophets employ to exploit gullible folks. It can help combat many superstitious and pseudoscientific claims and improve the quality of human life, knowledge, and ideas by ensuring the triumph of rationality and science over holy obscurantism and sacred folderol.

Humanism can allay the growing fear and anxiety for the future of the planet, and guarantee the future and survival of humanity, based on the principles and values of responsibility, sustainability, and stewardship, which it advocates.

In conclusion, humanism can help build a more humane society, where all human beings can make the best out of this life in the here and now. We can achieve a more meaningful and exuberant life and a happier and fulfilling existence, because this world is the only one we have.

6.

A SECULAR AND RELIGIOUS GUMBO, SERVED BROWN

Kenyatta Yamel

For many years the school boards of New York State thought that they were running churches rather than schools. Thanks to the state legislature, the schools were able to waste thousands of hours with so-called released-time policies. Under these schemes schoolchildren were sent from school to churches, synagogues, or other centers of religious brainwashing. I fought back.

I was born and raised in Buffalo, New York, a once-thriving city which has lost over two hundred thousand people in recent years. The city was and is rigidly segregated. One of the most effective means of segregation was in the building of its schools. In the second grade I attended School 93, which was located in a converted church. Attending School 93 meant walking eight blocks in the Black community, which was dangerous. A dog bit me once on the way to school. And the streets were full of cars driven by people with little regard, or so it seemed, for children.

The best thing I remember from those days was a kindly teacher named Mrs. Johnson, who looked like everyone's favorite grandmother. I imagined being swept up into her soft fluffiness and being read to in her home. If I could have remained in Mrs. Johnson's class all the time, I would have been enraptured. However, much to my surprise, I was assigned to something called "religious instruction" every Monday afternoon. I can recall being bundled off to a strange church which I had never seen before.

I was a young, shocked, colored boy. Because I was an early reader, I was told or asked to read Bible stories. I don't remember whether I refused. But I knew that no one asked my permission to assign me this class. I wanted to read about Dick and Jane. Where was Mrs. Johnson, and what did she have to do with this?

Rather than complaining to my mother and asking for her help in solving this problem, I kept to myself and asked the school officials what to do. Somehow, I think that I got removed from the class in either the third or fourth grade. The fourth grade was the most complicated of all. That was because my stepfather died and my mother used his insurance money to buy us a house. We moved ten blocks into a White neighborhood and a White school, where, much to my surprise, I found myself thrown into religious instruction once more.

This time I went straight to the principal's office and demanded to be permanently removed from the class. Furthermore, I "came out" at home, declaring that I had no use for God and even less for Christianity. This was not as difficult as it might seem. The church we had attended on holidays in the late 1950s and early 1960s had little to offer as far as I could tell. One of the churches had a gymnasium, but I did not feel comfortable with the other boys who played there. It was no place to be somebody.

As a small Black child, I was thrust into a situation which required speed for outrunning racist boys, good hand-eye coordination for fighting, and cleverness to avoid being kept after school. Once you were integrated into the White school, the system was designed to ensnare little Black boys like myself into detention, suspension, and being sent home. It was, as Gordon Parks would say, "a choice of weapons."

Appealing to God was not even considered as a solution to my problems. My reasoning told me that these were human problems and that I could apply logic to overcome them. Thus you could say I have always been a humanist, although I never read any humanist material until 1999. I was keenly aware of racial issues and the world around me. I remember watching an early episode of *Amos and Andy* and knowing instinctively that those characters did not reflect anything in my family.

I watched a television special, "Black History: Lost, Stolen, or Strayed," with my older sister Chris. I learned about the farm workers' struggles in California and joined the grape boycott. My interest in politics soon surpassed any interest that religion held for me. I developed close friendships with classmates and college students by participating in a liberal play, a movement to integrate the construction industry, and taking over campus offices. There was a famous picture from the University of Buffalo student protests in which I was running from tear gas with my books under my arm. There was a popular book published at the time called *Are You Running with Me, Jesus?* James Taylor wrote the song "Fire and Rain," which included a reference to Jesus. And there were other attempts to steer some of our youthful fervor into religion.

In my teens the church reentered the scene as a sanctuary for rambunctious youths. My younger brother James and I went to a coffeehouse in the basement of a Presbyterian church across the street from the University of Buffalo. I listened to antiwar songs and endless renditions of "The Great Mandala." I have no idea who the minister was or even the name of this church. What I respected was the willingness of the church to leave us alone and not to try and convert us to their beliefs.

I was also aware that some churches offered draft counseling and refuge for conscientious objectors. Although I would soon be subject to the draft, I did not use these services because I am not a conscientious objector. I progressed from supporting the president as a naive sophomore in high school to backing the Vietnamese in my senior year. In the high point of my activism from my teens to my mid-thirties, my belief in socialism sustained me. I was optimistic that the momentum of Vietnam, Angola, Mozambique, and Zimbabwe would continue to roll back capitalism.

I did not count on the loss of feelings of international solidarity. Maybe Americans never really united with these people, but were afraid of being killed. I never counted on the fall of the Berlin Wall and the collapse of the Soviet Union. I had always thought that somehow socialism and its ideal could be reformed and saved. I had, in short, a crisis of faith.

If I could not depend on the Party, could I depend on God? I started to attend churches that my politically active friends attended. I went to the Unitarian Church in Racine, Wisconsin, which had a very interesting and creative minister named Tony Larsen. I had shared the podium with him at a Central American protest, so I figured he was all right. I drifted away from the Unitarians when I moved to Milwaukee. I went to Our Savior's Lutheran Church for a few years and even liked the rituals. I thought that the story of Martin Luther attacking the hypocrites was wild. I even attended a nondenominational church called The Word Center where people spoke in tongues.

During this strange religious odyssey, I felt like an observer at a play, because despite wearing all these different religious cloaks, I was the same atheist I had always been. I remember a line from a song, "If you want to believe in something, why not believe in me?" Well, why not? You know, there's bound to be a nice Black girl at the church waiting for you. Why continue to remain apart? As practical as that might sound, I would still have to face my nine-year-old self who declared, "I don't believe in that stuff."

I have never been convinced of the existence of God or the idea that such a being actively participates in human events. Given such a belief, why should I attend church? Why not rejoin the Party or form a new party and put all my energies there? I got married in the Quaker Meetinghouse in Milwaukee about six years ago. The sanity of the Quaker silence was refreshing. I also needed to have a base with which to organize against the latest American wars. I survived the bloodiest era in the Third World since colonialism was established by talking and writing and holding onto friends. When I decided two or three years ago that the Quaker Meeting was like a steady diet of oat bran, I started attending the First Unitarian Society services. (You really should eat your oat bran, but can't we have a glass of wine and chocolate, too?)

The Unitarians helped introduce me to humanist writings, for which I am grateful. The writings of Corliss Lamont are the clearest I have ever read. And yet, as my minister Drew Kennedy would say, "We dare not fence the spirit." Apart from my early humanist leanings, I also felt that the man-made religious labels were artificial and served no purpose. After years of religious dabbling, I feel even more strongly that beneath those labels, we are all the same.

The Unitarian Universalists, while nondoctrinal, have a few basic beliefs that I share. These include

1. The inherent worth and dignity of every person.
2. Justice, equity, and compassion in human relations.
3. Acceptance of one another and encouragement to spiritual growth.
4. A free and responsible search for truth and meaning.
5. The rights of conscience and the use of the democratic process.
6. A goal of a world community with peace, liberty, and justice for all.
7. Respect and care for the interdependent web of all existence.

In practical terms, membership in the First Unitarian Society allowed me to help design and participate in several church services. I was part of a wonderful service about the life and work of Paul Robeson. I felt like Spike Lee in organizing a service in the summer of 1999 with two women, one from America's Black Holocaust Museum and the other from the American Jewish Committee. Opening music from Tuck and Patti and several gospel songs from an interracial choir organized by the Bahais rounded off the event.

I was also part of the humanist service which promoted the Humanist Ministries project I am helping to develop with my humanist friend Wendell Harris. We are moving forward with a plan to operate a group foster home for boys along humanist principles. The ministry will help me to pass along what I have learned to the next generation. When I hear the clowns in Congress talk about the need to promote values, I ask whose values. The values of a small minority of people who gained enormous economic and political advantage by exploiting the rest of the world? The values of a consumer culture which promotes the idea that having more and better goods will make us happy and make the economy grow? Or the values of the first and second humanist manifestos?

I am excited by the discussions in the humanist publications. The look of *Free Inquiry* excites me. Through a humanist friend, Carol Smith, I secured a free subscription to an online daily published by the American Atheists. Through its links to Congress, I have lobbied on some key issues. And I hope to use my position as the Program Chair of the Humanist Quest, a local affiliate of the American Humanist Association, to help make humanism visible in Milwaukee.

This is a large undertaking, but I am encouraged by Marge Piercy's poem "The Low Road." The last stanza says:

> It goes on one at a time
> it starts when you care
> to act, it starts when you do
> it again after they said no.
> it starts when you say We
> and know who you mean, and each
> day you mean one more.*

---

*From *The Moon Is Always Female*, by Marge Piercy, copyright © 1980 by Marge Piercy. Used by permission of Alfred A. Knopf, a division of Random House, Inc.

7.

"MY LORD, I WANT TO GO AND THINK" (Choosing Reason Over Faith)

Leo Igwe

I was born into a Catholic family. My parents were not very committed churchgoers. While my mother in every sense could be described as very religious, my father was apathetic at best or even hypocritical about religious matters. But they ensured I had a typical Catholic upbringing. We went to church every Sunday, and said the nightly prayers almost every day and did the Stations of the Cross each Lenten season. They also tried to enforce the prayer-before-meal ritual, and on several occasions interrupted my meal so that I could say the grace. As a child I found this distasteful and disagreeable.

As a great devotee of the Virgin Mary, my mother made sure we recited the rosary very often, particularly in the months of May and October. Saying the rosary was an agonizing experience for me, and I always wished that the months of May and October would never come. However, at some stage I had to develop a tactic. Most often I caught part of my sleep in the course of the prayers. In the name of prayers my parents tried to inculcate a lot of outrageous values—self-ishness, fear, hatred, and suspicion—into me. Our prayers were always for our own life, progress, health, and well-being, and for the safety and protection of our family from the snares and evil plots of our numerous enemies. They made me understand that a lot of people hated us and were after us to kill us, to poison us, to thwart our progress, and to annihilate us completely. My father used his prayers to insult and oppress my mother or to castigate, reprimand, or intimidate everybody. His often long intercessions were fraught with dirty, indecent, and vulgar language.

I never saw anything moral about praying in this manner. I hated prayers and couldn't see the need for praying in the first place. Prayers were not solving our family problems. They never stopped my father from beating my mother, or prevented him from fighting with his brothers. I started longing for a time I would live without praying.

At age twelve I was sent to the seminary, primarily to be disciplined and never, I can recall vividly, to prepare for the priesthood. In the seminary, it was praying, praying all the time, at least eight times every day. Prayer was one of those rules and formalities one must fulfill in order to stay. Hence I prayed not because I knew I was talking to a god or goddess but because it was compulsory. I prayed for the sake of the rule, not because I believed. My studies in philosophy at the seminary exposed me to the thought and writings of famous thinkers and scholars such as Pythagoras, Socrates, Plato, Aristotle, Hume, Mill, Heidegger, Freud, Russell, and others, and equipped me with critical-thinking skills. They offered me a veritable opportunity to try, test, question, and examine in the light of reason most of the traditional religious views, presumptions, and postulations—the idea of God, the deity's lofty attributes, revelation, salvation, prophecy, holiness, sin, fasting, blessing, immortality, heaven, hell, and so forth.

I came to the conclusion that religion was a product of human fantasy, unreason, and fanaticism, articulated, fabricated, and institutionalized to enslave, manipulate, and exploit the weak, the ignorant, and the feebleminded. I came to understand more vividly what Karl

Marx meant when he called religion the "opium of the people," "the sigh of the oppressed creature, the breath of a breathless world, the soul of a soulless condition." Moreover, I learned why Bertrand Russell delineated and described religion as harmful and obstructive to human and moral well-being and progress.

I was particularly stunned by the magnitude of "god-playing" that went on in the name of faith and piety. Whenever the priests and the bishops said anything, they would say, "God said," "God told me"—as if God talks. There was a case of a seminarian who, when he was about to be expelled, was told by his bishop, "My son, the Holy Spirit is not calling you." Who is the Holy Spirit? The Bishop. The priests. I found this very revolting, unacceptable, and demoralizing, and I couldn't understand why somebody would attribute a decision made by human beings to a phantom Holy Spirit. The very painful aspect of it all is that nobody dared to oppose, object to, or challenge these flagrant pronouncements. But at some point I started raising objections. I started demanding rational justifications of those bogus Catholic dogmas. One time was during a psychology class. Our lecturer (a priest) told us that we should go and pray whenever we felt sexually aroused. And I had to put it to him that "since whenever we are hungry we go and eat and whenever we are thirsty we go and drink, why should we go and pray when we feel sexually aroused?" He said it was because as celibates, our sexual passions are sacrificed to God. I knew this was not true and that many of our priests and religious folk take care of themselves in a "holy way."

This was not going down well with me. I couldn't imagine myself as a priest, a revered father ordained to peddle, propagate, and preach this gospel of lies, deceit, and hypocrisy. I started considering seriously an alternative—a life not only outside the seminary and the Catholic Church, but outside religion as a whole—a life freed from the shackles of faith and dogma. Rather than accepting the saying if you can't beat them join them, I opted for if you can't beat them leave them.

Hence one morning I walked straight to my bishop and told him, "My Lord, I want to go and think." Since then, I have never returned. Having bid farewell to God and religion, I have pitched my tent with humanism.

Humanism has reinforced my belief in freedom, reason, hard work, knowledge, and creativity. By making me the master of my life, by making me the architect of my fate and destiny, the humanist eupraxophy has helped transform what would have been a life of despair, pessimism, cynicism, and passivism into one of hope, optimism, positivism, and activism.

Humanism can be of enormous benefit to all of humankind. As an alternative to traditional religions, humanism provides humanity with an intellectual and philosophical antidote to the religious poisoning, madness, brainwashing, and indoctrination going on around the world today, particularly in Africa. It imbues the individual with self-belief, self-esteem, courage, and confidence to confront and overcome the problems and challenges of life, enabling every person to realize his or her unique vision of the good life. Humanism banishes fear, despair, and a sense of guilt and sin which religion employs to belittle and hold down the human personality.

Humanism uplifts and facilitates the total and unhindered development and realization of all human potential. By tackling the intellectual roots of poverty, conflicts, and underdevelopment, humanism can help broaden the circle of peace, prosperity, dignity, and opportunity for all, regardless of race, sex, religion, and ethnic or national origin.

With its emphasis on free and critical inquiry, humanism can protect the human mind against error, myth, and superstition, liberating it from suffocating orthodoxies, stifling dogmas, and nonsense. In addition, humanism advocates open moral and sex education, access to birth control and family planning—the use of contraceptives and abortion—and therefore can help humanity curb population growth, unwanted pregnancies, and the spread of STDs and AIDS.

Furthermore, humanism values and cherishes the interdependence and interconnectedness of all life-forms and the need for the sustainable use and preservation of the Earth's resources for future generations. As such, humanism can help humankind control environmental pollution and degradation, check global warming, and reduce ozone-layer depletion and the destruction of biodiversity.

As a philosophy that aims to build common ground and promote tolerant pluralism, humanism can help humanity overcome the racial discrimination, ethnic hatred and genocide, religious intolerance and fanaticism, sexual violence, gender inequality, and insensitivity that plague and plunder many nations and societies in our contemporary world.

Finally, humanism can provide our increasingly interdependent world with a realistic global ethics for the construction of a true planetary society based on shared values.

8.

ASCENSION TO HUMANISM

Keenya H. Oliver

I have always had a natural curiosity about the world and our place in it. My father often took me to the American Museum of Natural History in Manhattan and encouraged me to watch nature programs. I also enjoyed learning about science in school. These early experiences with science would introduce me to something called "critical thinking." Science, the best explainer of natural phenomena available to mankind, demands a critical examination in the world. The knowledge from critical examination is then used (one way or another) to manipulate nature. My parents, both professionals, were quite influential in my understanding of the importance of critical thinking.

On the other hand, I, like many other kids and adults, was also prone to "magical thinking." That thump in the night might be a ghost or a monster. Nothing happens by accident. A chance meeting is no coincidence. Magical thinking was even encouraged by adults in the form of a favorite childhood "harmless" myth—Santa Claus. As a child, it seemed conceivable that a plump, robber-baron-looking, old man could deliver toys to all the children of the world in twenty-four hours. I thought programs that presented only the paranormal point of view, such as the "Man Who Saw Tomorrow" about Nostradamus, were documentaries. It certainly *looked* like a documentary, with a narrator and "facts." I remember that I cried during the part that depicted the great cities of the world blowing up, because it seemed like proof that the world would end.

However, for as long as I could remember, I was also logical and analytical. If a story did not make logical sense, I was troubled by it. My inherent logic also led me to ask questions that many would object to being asked. I wondered why these "documentaries" were so one-sided, and why fortune-tellers were not wealthy. There were elements of the Santa Claus story that bothered me as a child. I remember being surprised to find out from a Jewish girl in my first-grade class that not everyone celebrated Christmas. How did Santa know which kids were Christian and which were not? I lived in an apartment building, so the method Santa used to enter the apartment without a chimney was always a mystery. I found the adult responses to the question somewhat unsatisfactory. The toys also looked surprisingly store-bought; did Santa shop at Macy's too? Of course, I still accepted Santa because adults insisted that he was real, and I was credulous. Nonetheless, I was bothered by these logical problems. It took one encounter with a grade-school classmate to find out the truth about Santa. That was one of my first experiences of having an erroneous belief challenged.

This fearlessness for asking tough questions would lead me to doubts about even bigger beliefs. I never was a Bible-toting Christian, but I did accept the Judeo-Christian God I was raised to believe in. My ascension to humanism was slow and arduous, but nonetheless, reason prevailed. I was bothered by the anthropomorphism in the Bible. God seems all too human—jealous, vengeful, and far too interested in the minutiae of our sex lives. I also wondered where non-human animals fit in morality arguments. One issue centers on the

Argument from Evil; how do we explain the bad things that happen to other animals? Certainly, nonhuman animals neither commit the all-too-human atrocities that allegedly keep us in sin, nor will they grow up to do so. However, quite a few of our fellow terrestrials are sentient and capable of suffering. Why should the evils inflicted on us affect them? It wasn't until I read about Darwin's doubt years later that I found an in-depth discussion of this point of view. Not only is the Bible anthropocentric, but also literally centers on the male sex. In the second chapter of Genesis, Eve was created after man and the animals, showing her status in society from creation. She was also responsible for the downfall of mankind and was subject to harsher punishment. Speaking of "the fall," I always wondered why we should have to be punished for the sins of our forefathers; don't we each have our own free will? The Bible has often been used to defend the subjugation of women.

I remember discussing the Design Argument for God's existence with a friend of mine in high school. The argument seemed convincing enough, until it was brought to its logical conclusion. If everything that exists needs a creator, then who created God? How can God be left uncreated? Ultimately we are left with an uncaused cause, which defeats the argument. Why do we need God to begin with? Could we not conclude that because God can be left uncaused, the universe could also be left uncaused? I realized, "*Who* created the universe?" was an inappropriate question. I would later find out that this is a form of begging the question; the more appropriate question would be, "Does the universe *have* a creator?" Of course, the theistic responses to the question were unsatisfactory. I was even told that it is an inappropriate question, one that is too blasphemous to ask. I found that peculiar; why would such a powerful deity care if someone questioned the circumstances underlying his existence, especially in light of the evidence (or lack thereof) he left?

Inquiry should be opened; how can a person expect to discover the truth without asking honest questions? One reason empirical tests are so successful is that they eliminate bias. If we are truly interested in finding out the truth, we must do our best to eliminate wishful thinking and conjecture. The inclusion of controls and blind testing in empirical design is the best method we have of eliminating such biases. Most of us understand the importance of testing in everyday life. After all, no one would accept "I have a good feeling" as evidence that that car on the showroom floor works. We want to go out and test-drive the car, and even possibly have a mechanic look at it. But when it comes to the paranormal, that importance is too often forgotten.

Any inquiry with limits is not free; it is stifled. Why should we be afraid to ask questions about our most fundamental beliefs? One important aspect of scientific investigation is falsification. A hypothesis must be falsifiable—in other words, the hypothesis must be able to be false. In order for a hypothesis to be verifiable, it must have the ability to be tested. Not only does the hypothesis have to be testable, but it must also be replicable. Others must be able to achieve the same results so we can have confidence about its reliability. If the hypothesis is tested, stands up to scrutiny after multiple tests, and is not rejected, the hypothesis survives. The existence of supernatural deities cannot be tested and therefore lies outside the realm of falsification. How would the God hypothesis possibly be rejected? One major problem is what would count as evidence against God's existence; theists routinely try to explain away any refutations. There should be a clear-cut way to reject the hypothesis, but there cannot be if an acceptable reply to the negative is, "The Lord works in mysterious ways." The above underlies the fear behind not allowing the ultimate creator question to be asked. To maintain such a belief in our society, critical thinking about the deity must be discouraged. If believers were encouraged to think deeply about this proof, it could cause doubt and weaken belief. However, in our modern, scientific society, people understand the importance of having evidence for a belief. Consequences must be invented to discourage those questions. Possible punishment from the particular Almighty will suffice. Most of the time, theists are not open to the idea that God does not exist. Belief in God is unquestionably true and any evidence that may be contrary is reinterpreted to fit the "fact" of God's existence.

I am often accused by theists/believers of the paranormal of not having an open mind. "Isn't it possible there are phenomena out there that we cannot explain?" they decry. "Aren't there things that go beyond human understanding?" some have asked me. Of course I accept that there are many mysteries that remain unsolved, even some that perhaps go beyond the limits of our brains. However, I do not fall back on a paranormal cushion. History has shown that apparently paranormal phenomena had quite natural explanations that were not understood at the time. Disease, such as the black plague, was caused not by demons, but by microorganisms that we could not see with our naked eye. Part of open-mindedness is being open to the possibility of being wrong. Our minds cannot be open if we start with the pretense that our belief cannot be false. I accept that there are things we do not yet know, but that does not mean that the unknown is necessarily paranormal. Skeptic Society director Michael Shermer refers to this as putting God in the gaps of our knowledge. We humans seem very uncomfortable with the unknown. Filling in the unknown gaps with the paranormal superficially seems like a satisfactory explanation, but we have simply replaced one mystery with another.

Why is "I don't know" not a sufficient answer? There is also another essential principle in the sciences called Occam's razor, which states that the simplest explanation is usually the correct one. All we have is the real world, so we have no reason to believe that the explanation will lie outside it. A paranormal explanation such as an uncaused God who created the universe, but did not leave convincing evidence of it, adds on unnecessary extras; it is much simpler to say the universe does not need a causal explanation. It seems safe to assume that the same natural laws have always governed the universe, and we should not abandon the possibility of a natural explanation unless we have a solid reason for doing so. As the late, great astronomer Carl Sagan stated, "Extraordinary claims need extraordinary proof."

I still clung to religion and the Judeo-Christian God for comfort. I have often heard it is better to believe, because it is comforting in an unpredictable world. It would be comforting to know that there is a being out there who cares and interferes on behalf of our well-being. Church often serves as a stress reliever for African Americans and other oppressed people who must deal with the many repressive "-isms" in our society. We want to think the universe cares about each of us. We would like to think there is a messiah out there who will punish the oppressor and relieve the oppressed. However, upon further inspection, I found belief in this deity not comforting, but alarming. How can one find comfort in worshiping an omnipotent, omnibenevolent being who essentially does not interfere with our universe? How can we reconcile the presence of such a being and the unfairness of our world? After all, it is not uncommon for the innocent to suffer and the despicable to reign. There is an obvious paradox. The idea that God is all-powerful and all-good is incompatible with our existing world. If he is all-good and all-powerful, then he has the power to prevent such atrocities, but does nothing. If he is not all-powerful and/or all-good, he is powerless to stop it and we cannot hope for his help. Worse yet, the God of the Bible is jealous, tyrannical, vengeful, and allows those in his favor to commit acts many would find repulsive. Is such a being really worthy of our worship?

Nonetheless, it is still difficult to give up these beliefs, particularly the ones we're raised with. I still tried to hold onto belief in Santa, even when I knew it did not make logical sense. It was hard to accept that those in authority, particularly parents, can be wrong. However, they knew Santa was only a myth; but many adults truly believe there is a God. It took me a long time to realize that I had to let go of God. It was not until I was referred to as an atheist while discussing the topic that I recognized I *was* one. God and religion held less and less importance in my life, until finally I let it go. I still held on because I was "supposed" to believe, but the theistic position became less defensible over time. Logic won out over emotion in my case.

We cannot prove (or disprove) God any more than we can prove Santa Claus. Both are untestable hypotheses. The refutation of theism is indirect. We can test certain empirical claims for a God's existence, such as the biblical creationist claim of a global flood. Those arguments which lie outside the scientific sphere are still subject to logical scrutiny. Theistic proofs of a god, such as the First Cause or the Argument from Design, can be explained in simpler, naturalistic ways. The more we discover about the universe, the more the gaps close. Undoubtedly our current gaps will close with continuing scientific discovery. The more I learned about the world, the more unnecessary the God explanation became. Rather than being frightened by a life not designated by a grand designer, I was liberated by the autonomy of my own thoughts—my own free will. I am not the mere automaton of some super, unknowable deity—I am in complete control of my life, free to control my own destiny. In a sense, the human race is like the egocentric child who thinks the world was made just for him or her. Only recently have we begun to rise out of the egocentrism. We are a part of nature and not above it. We live on a small planet, orbiting an average star on the outskirts of a not-so-extraordinary galaxy. If we were to go back in time and start life on Earth over again, the outcome would most likely be very different. That makes our existence even more extraordinary to me. It is more parsimonious to say that nature is all we need, in fact, all we know of for sure. I am an atheist in the sense that I have no belief in a deity. In fact, it seems more likely that we invented our own gods to explain the unknown, and to enforce appropriate conduct. There is no need to postulate extraordinary paranormal beings when we already have this wonderfully extraordinary universe. How can I worry about the next *possible* life that no one is certain exists, when there is so much to attend to in *this* lifetime? Our universe is enough.

9.

THINKING BACK

Anthony B. Pinn

I joined the Church, found salvation, and entered the ministry early. By the time I was a teenager, I had preached in various churches, participated in revivals, and, according to some, I showed great promise. This potential, or "preacher look," was well captured in the energetic style of expression, complete with "dancing in the spirit" and "speaking in tongues" that bore evidence of my commitment to God and an embrace of the Holy Spirit. Although the style of my religious expression and exhortation was somewhat energized and flexible because I desired to be "open to the leadings of the Spirit," my religiosity was doctrinally guarded and rigid. Underlying my articulation of "the faith" was an unquestionable appeal to the Truth of the scripture: "The Bible says. . . ." My rather immature perception of the Christian faith did not seriously entertain difficult questions, the questions raised by the existential dilemmas associated with Black life in White America.

At that stage I never would have held God accountable in any serious way for the sufferings of the oppressed. Such questioning would have bordered on faithlessness or disobedience. Like Augustine, I thought of humanity as flawed and struggling for closeness to God, life in a very spiritualized sense. I thought of human progress and accomplishment as a direct result of God's goodness. God, not humanity, served as the measure of all things. My religious sensibilities forced history to conform to church doctrine.

If this rather unreflective approach to religion had been confined to my young, preteen years, it could easily be dismissed as the perspective of a child. But I held it far too long to receive that type of sympathy.

My schooling, from third grade through ninth, had taken place within the context of the program for the gifted within the city of Buffalo, New York. Yet for a young Christian preacher determined to avoid the temptations of the world, the permissiveness and secularity of the Special Progress program was too much. After all, Scripture indicated that I should be "in the world but not of it," including the avoidance of "all appearances of evil." I was convinced that obedience to these scriptural admonishments required separation from "worldly" classmates and curricula that did not reflect the Truth of the Gospel message. There was no latitude with respect to morals—not in my world. So I left and enrolled in West Seneca Christian School, a small Southern Baptist, church-affiliated school.

For many students, I was the first African American with whom they spent any significant time. For most, their perception of African Americans was based on "stories of the inner city" and stereotypical television characters, peppered with local racist leanings. All of this was couched in a rather sterile and rigid form of Christianity. In a word, this high school fed students into Bob Jones University. Enough said.[1]

I learned several things from attending West Seneca Christian School. Among these various lessons was the realization that Christians come in a variety of forms—some of them crude and racist.

These "Christians," at least in their interactions with me, often hid their racial biases and ignorance under a thin crust of religious ritual and rhetoric. Often the crust cracked.

The three years I spent commuting to West Seneca Christian opened my eyes to the nasty underbelly of Christianity, the manner in which its doctrine easily supported less-than-honorable activities and opinions. But my faith remained.

It was not until I left Buffalo for Columbia University that I was exposed to a study of history and culture that did not shy away from a critique of the Christian tradition. This was initially troubling, based on the indoctrination of the previous three years. West Seneca Christian School promoted conformity to a warped Christian vision, and at Columbia all of that and more was brought into question in what I consider relatively healthy and useful ways. I wanted this challenge, but I was far from prepared for it. Before my arrival in New York City I based my response to questions on scriptural Truth, and this worked because I dismissed anyone who did not understand the word of God as the primary source of truth. At this point I began a move toward intellectual curiosity and hard questions related to my religious beliefs.

I remember one episode in particular. Over dinner in the cafeteria, a good friend asked me if I believed in the virgin birth of Christ—a quick questioning of my literal reading of Scripture and one of its foundational claims. I, assuming this would be an opportunity to testify, answered quickly in the affirmative. Following my confident and energetic reply, he systematically brought into question the "truth" of Scripture and the possibility of Mary's conception of Jesus through sexual intercourse. His was a reading of Scripture based on a hermeneutic of suspicion and science, mine a hermeneutic of loyalty.

My initial response was to console myself by arguing that my friend was going to hell, but I could not dismiss him and his argument that cavalierly. I forced myself to bracket (as best I could) my self-righteous impulse and think.

My sense of religious devotion was changing, and my idea of the essential nature of Scripture (as history) for religious life was altered. I became more willing to bring Scripture and Christian doctrine into relationship with historical happenings and sociopolitical—and also cultural—developments of the twentieth century. My theoretical and methodological framework grew in complexity. I was beginning to open to liberation theology and its preoccupation with human experience as the measure of theological truth. This theological turn helped me as I struggled to maintain a tension to keep my Christian commitment, but in light of historical experience. I continued thinking through this tension as I moved from Columbia University to graduate work at Harvard University.

I was going to Harvard to train for the ministry, to get the credentials and information necessary to be successful in the pastorate. I was not fully prepared for the Harvard environment. I assumed it would be similar to Columbia, but I also assumed that as a divinity school, it would be a large group of Christians sharing and growing together. What I encountered was an approach to religious faith that did not entail the religious limitations I took for granted. For me, this time during my Master of Divinity training was a guilty pleasure. I welcomed the challenges and exposure although, at times, I felt I should not.

The decision to remain at Harvard for doctoral work was fairly easy. I had the opportunity to continue thinking about my understanding of God and my relationship to the Christian faith. And with the encouragement of faculty, I began to question some of my basic and ill-reasoned assumptions, based on a growing body of resources and experiences.

Much of my change took place through an unwavering look at theodicy: What can we say about the justice of God in light of human suffering? I was convinced this was the central issue. Once resolved, all other elements of a working faith would fall in place. My movements toward humanism were powerful but small. My first inclination, using theodicy, was simply to assert that humans misunderstand the nature of God's interaction with humans. Drawing on Barth, I asserted that we cannot know the mind of God, therefore human suffering does not make sense to us. This, however, does not bring into question the goodness and justice of God. Rather, it is an indictment of our own inadequacies. This position did not last long—perhaps one of my eight years at Harvard.

My new assertion was that we humans misunderstand God's involvement in the world. We assume that God is responsible for bringing freedom and liberation when in fact we must work with God to achieve a transformed society, because God has placed a limitation on God's self out of respect for free will. When social transformation does not take place, it is because we have fallen short. This argument formed the basis of my master's thesis. I was slowly moving toward an atheistic humanism.

I became somewhat disillusioned with my resolution to the problem of evil (theodicy). I began to wonder: perhaps there is no evidence of God's involvement in the struggle against oppression because there is no God. Perhaps such struggles are questionable at best because humans struggle alone. The symbol God (there is nothing else to God but this symbolic importance) had outlived its usefulness. I had not based this emerging humanism on Renaissance or Enlightenment literature. Rather, it was based on facing the harshness of human behavior and the absurd nature of human interactions. Finally, I began to look at racism, sexism, and other forms of oppression without retreat to religious platitudes.

This opinion was unpopular, even with some of my more liberal and suspicious conversation partners. For some, their continued concern with church involvement made such a position indefensible. Although occasional doubts surfaced, I continued to hold this position, convinced that it was not only reasonable but truthful.

Flawed concepts of God are not the only avenue into humanism; the constellation of humanist possibilities is too extensive for that. Yet it allowed me to make sense of the world and articulate an identity that was not defined by mythic contact between God and humans. It acknowledged the risks involved in living and embraced these risks, realizing that life without them is subhuman.

I graduated still holding this humanist position, but in conversation with a range of perspectives found within my communities of concern. In short, mine is a humanism in dialogue; that is to say, I have no personal belief in a divine, removed, or transcendent reality. Yet I remain intrigued by what may come from respectful dialogue with those who do. The goal for me is to avoid a form of fundamentalist humanism that is as rigid and inflexible as the Christian fundamentalism I oppose. That is to say, I am unwilling to assert my humanism in a way that prevents an informative exchange with those who hold other perspectives. This means that I posit my claims as one response to the quest for identity and meaning. I consider it an important position—one with benefit—and I want to expose its value. While I understand that this includes critical reflection on other structures of belief, I want to provide this analysis as a call for conversation, not exclusion.

Reflecting on my days in the church journeying to my current position of humanism, I would "take nothing for my journey," in the words of the Church folk. It has been a matter of important existential wrestling, and I'm pleased with the sense of individual and community identity forged. In fact, I often think to myself about the benefits of the humanist perspective: it forces a strong sense of accountability and responsibility for our actions and inactivities. This is not to say humanism is problem-free. No, humanists are also capable of horrific deeds. Yet, humanism does open the possibility of renewal in profound and challenging ways.

NOTE

1. *Editor's note:* Bob Jones University is a thoroughly reactionary institution of higher education in Greenville, South Carolina. The first Black student was not admitted until the 1970s, and the school finally lifted its ban on interracial dating in March 2000.

10.

FROM SUPERNATURALISM TO AGNOSTICISM

David Stewart Summers

God, in the words of Anne Ridler, seems "mute & deaf & dead indeed." It (not "he" or "she") or "god" is a concept, an idea (and far from an ideal), an invention or literary character, perpetuated by imaginative minds down through the ages, and subsequently imposed with a motive of mind and body and village and state and eventually even world control. And nobody perceived these truths better than Thomas Jefferson, Thomas Paine, and James Madison in the eighteenth century and Ludwig Feuerbach and Robert Ingersoll in the nineteenth century. All religions, in the words of a freethought Mormon who had been excommunicated for his stand against the policy of the Church excluding Negroes from the priesthood, "bind the mind and drown the conscience" (John W. Fitzgerald). On planet Earth certainly, more than enough tragedy is maintained through natural disasters, so humankind should minimize, not augment, the forces of evil and suffering. I agree with the observation by Emerson, "It is the highest duty that [humankind] should be honored in us," and the beacon for uplifting humankind is humanism, not the sweeping irrational impositions of the "god" concept, of which all faiths or religions are guilty.

My introduction to supernaturalism occurred literally at birth, since both of my parents were devout Christians; from the formative years I recall regular church services, daily parental prayers, and multiple eulogies for the dead, with the most vivid funerals being those of my mother (who died at age twenty-seven), both paternal grandparents, and several of my father's friends, all of whom expired before I was six years old. That I was skeptical about Christianity, even at two or three years of age, was probably inherent or genetic; like Henry David Thoreau, "I was not born to be forced [but would] breathe after my own fashion." And clearly there is no greater force or "tyranny over the mind of [humankind]" than that of faith or religion, which currently, incidentally, threatens the very survival of democracy in America through fanatical right-wing forces. At age thirteen I became a "converted member" of a Baptist church, but even then I disbelieved the "Satan and hell" stories, while remaining skeptical about "God and heaven and immortality." Simultaneously I also realized that my dear uncle, Wade Freeman of Rappahannock County, Virginia, was not a church member, yet he was one of the kindest and most highly respected persons I had ever known, exceeded in my esteem only by my father.

In Canton, Ohio, the place of my birth, my parents had been two of the founders of Bethel C.M.E. ("Christian Methodist Episcopal") Church, August 19, 1931; the facility remains operational today, having celebrated fifty years of service in 1981. Following my mother's death in 1935, my two sisters and three brothers were brought to Rappahannock County, Virginia, to live with our uncle and aunt, Wade & Madaline Freeman; I was left for three years with my father (who would die in 1963), who chose to remain in Canton for the benefit of higher wages at Republic Steel Corporation. Thus from three to six years of age, before and after my mother's death, I had playmates from many ethnic groups, including other African Americans, Greeks, Portuguese, Irish, Germans, Italians, and both southern and northern, indigenous American Caucasians, all of whom were friends through innocence, naturally requiring that critical amount of time before learning racism from society. But my mother especially instilled in us both a reverence for God and respect for all humans, skin pigmentation notwithstanding. In later years, when my father became aware of my convictions about evolution and the "interpretive" rather than "realistic" aspects of biblical creation, he reemphasized that I must never forget the importance of God in life's journey, and reminded me again at my graduation from medical school in 1959. But I could not forget the unanswered plea of my mother, who from the combined effects of her faith and poverty, had prayed for good health rather than seeking medical attention for what she perceived to be heart disease. Her death in March 1935, when I was three years old, is the most likely cause of my annual melancholy—an irresistible pervasive sadness which invades my consciousness every spring and Christmas, originating, no doubt, from a subconscious level. But I also have a conscious recollection of my mother, not only from the agonizing domain of her funeral but also from the comforting consolation of her arms when I was crying, probably before I was three years old, and during her illness when she would beg for quiet.

In my progression from toleration of supernaturalism (for certainly it was toleration rather than conviction) to agnosticism and humanism, I am indebted partly to my exposure to the history of the Church of Jesus Christ of Latter Day Saints; partly to LDS beliefs, conceived through Joseph Smith's imagination or dreams or epileptic hallucinations or fabrications;[1] and partly to my "state-side foreign service" in Salt Lake City from 1972 to 1976. It was my comparison of the Book of Mormon with biblical stories which instigated my realization or enlightenment of the fact that both the Bible and the Book of Mormon were created, ordained, and sustained by none other than *Homo sapiens*, i.e., by multiple predominantly male and nondivine dreamers in mental tyranny for the Bible, and singularly by Joseph Smith for the Book of Mormon. Initially in 1972, after the President of the LDS Church, Harold B. Lee, proclaimed on television that he "was waiting for the Lord to tell him what to do" regarding the denial of the priesthood to Blacks, I considered his comment blasphemous, non-Christian, defiling and racist, since the Lord had told Christians what to do almost two thousand years before then. On April 15, 1974, these thoughts were expressed in my letter to the next president, Spencer W. Kimball, and in many follow-up letters I encouraged him to end the shamelessly racist policy, but the response was always, "We acknowledge receipt of your letter." Copies of my letters were mailed repeatedly to various political, educational, and religious leaders throughout America, with the hope that President Kimball and his hierarchy would expedite the "revelation" whereby "the Lord" would concur that equality and harmony among human brothers should be neither delayed, distorted, nor suppressed. My family and I left Utah in August 1976, but on June 9, 1978, President Kimball's expedient and political "divinity" and mind finally lifted the ban on Blacks holding the priesthood; in a letter to him dated June 20, 1978, I congratulated him on behalf of "the handful of contemporary Black Mormons" and again invited him to reflect on Emerson's powerful discourse on Reform, while striving even further for racial harmony.

If history is "an agreed-upon set of fabrications," controlled by power and culture and prevailing pedagogic concepts (instead of reality and truth and the restraints of reason), then certainly the Bible is at best "history"—inherently erroneous in chronology, opinion, and epistemology—and at worst an "indulgence in the illusions of hope" (the words are Patrick Henry's), a surrender to supernaturalism, a pretension of God's existence, and an exploitation of first millennial ignorance, second millennial mind control, and humankind's perpetual "yearning of the soul for the realm of [a] Divine." And what is true for the Bible and the Book of Mormon regarding a supposed "word of God" is also true for all other so-called sacred texts. Throughout my life and even during early childhood Sunday School sessions in Washington (Rappahannock County), Virginia, and later in Williamsburg, Virginia, during my high-school years, I always questioned the claims of Christianity as contrasted with the dogma of other religions. Finally becoming convinced that all could not be correct, and since all religions obviously have false claims, not unlike Thomas Paine in his 1794 book *The Age of Reason*, "I disbelieve them all." Both biblical fallacy and human gullibility probably contribute to the current degree of American fanaticism, with its threat to the First Amendment separation of church and state. The simultaneous imposition of "creation science," posting of the Ten Commandments, vouchers for sectarian schools, and other Catholic and Christian Right schemes for tearing down the "wall of separation between church and state" are also undermining the stability of American democracy, which both Jefferson and Lincoln conceived as "the last best hope of earth." The idea of an American theocracy must be recognized for its inherent dangers, by which faith by force or Inquisitions of Catholicism could again destroy America's freedoms, while the ignorance-based attacks on evolution and the scientific method can lead only to a pre-Galileo national mentality. The glory of science is its ability to annihilate delusion and ignorance while unveiling truth.

What, then, is the promise of humanism or objectivism or the free-inquiry essence of agnosticism in my philosophy? First, I must not deny that humankind is part and parcel of "that Great Nature which embosoms us all," in the words of Emerson, making it foolhardy for me to aspire toward ultimate happiness or self-improvement in some unknown and unexpected future realm. Not only must we die as inhabitants of planet Earth but we must also live until that final breath, and during our visit we must agree with Ingersoll that "happiness is the only good," not "by and by" but *now*, not in an imaginary heaven but *here*, and "the way to be happy is to make others so." The sooner humankind accepts these truths of our fate on Earth, the earlier we may anticipate genuine and sustained happiness, with scientific and technological advancement for all of the world's humans. And pretensions among multiple and various religions that the right creed for living is *Dieu lo vuit* (God wills it) must be acknowledged for what they are—appeals to the unknown, exploitations of fear, projections of the human psyche, or poetic expressions of yearning and longing. As depicted by Gibran, our *daily lives* must be both "our temple *and* our religion" into which we should "take *all* [humankind]: for in adoration [we] cannot fly higher than their hopes nor humble [ourselves] lower than their despair." Humanism, which in my view is not a religion and should not attempt to emulate the predominating and evil religions of the world, is the foremost philosophy by which humankind may uphold democratic government—or government in which freedom FROM religion becomes "the last best hope of earth." And it is with a resounding affirmation of humanism that humankind may answer Emerson's eternal rhetorical question:

> What is man born for but to be a Reformer; a Remaker of what man has made; a Renouncer of lies; a Restorer of truth and good—imitating that Great Nature which embosoms us all and which sleeps no moment on an old past but every hour Repairs herself, yielding us every hour a new day and with every pulsation, a new life?!

NOTE

1. Fawn M. Brodie, *No Man Knows My History; The Life of Joseph Smith, the Mormon Prophet*, 2d ed., rev. and enl. (New York: Knopf, 1971), pp. 405–21.

11.

THE CATHOLIC EDUCATION OF AN ATHEIST

Patrick Inniss

Black atheist—now there's a term that can push a lot of buttons. If you were to compile a list of noncriminal characteristics with nevertheless negative connotations, the words "Black" and "atheist" would have to be included. These are also words that describe me.

I've always been Black, but I haven't always been an atheist. I was raised a Roman Catholic. Being a good Catholic may have given me exactly the insights I needed to become an atheist. I certainly wouldn't want to have missed that.

Racism and religion have been two of the most significant institutions in American society. Being a Black atheist provides a unique perspective, especially if one has also experienced religion as well. Black people tend to have sophisticated and well-formed notions concerning race, indicative of the time most have spent pondering that subject since an early age. Similarly, atheists are often more informed on religious subjects than their Bible-believing counterparts. And both Black people and atheists are outsiders.

Black people and atheists may both be disfavored minorities, but in that same unsophisticated and anachronistic mind-set they are not linked in any other way. On the contrary, godlessness is one of the few negative traits *not* commonly assigned to Blacks. Atheists are imagined to be heartless, overintellectualized eggheads who are probably Communists or ethnically Jewish, or maybe both. Blacks, on the other hand, would have a natural devotion to God that is a product of their lack of education and innate childlike simplemindedness. The concept of a Black atheist would demand the destruction of either one stereotype or the other.

The way Black people have traditionally been portrayed in the media and literature follows along these lines: If we weren't eating watermelons, snoozing in the middle of the afternoon, or playing dice, then likely as not we would be singing ourselves hoarse at some holyroller church. Blacks are often depicted as relying upon their faith and religious institutions to cope with the considerable impediments which have been placed in their way. Victims need faith. The helpless and hopeless need faith. The less able are almost expected to appeal to a "higher power" to guide them through this bewildering world.

Given the preconception that Black people are by nature religious, when people find out that I am an atheist they often seem to take a moment for error checking. Some basic principle has been violated and an incorrect result produced. It's almost as if I had said that I'm a poor dancer. To some extent even Black people buy into this perspective. The surprised reaction in response to my atheism does not vary much by race. But Black people don't necessarily feel like victims, or at any real disadvantage in their relationship with the world. Although suffering through massive exposure to the malady of religious thinking, some have emerged uninfected.

This is not to say that religion isn't a big influence in Black society. It is. Religion is always more important to people of lesser political and economic means. Despite this, there is also a significant history of freethought among Black people. The existence of powerful and active churches in the Black community is a reflection more of imposed socioeconomic factors than of any inherent religiosity on the part of Black people. Instances of corruption and abuse within the Black church have cultivated a strain of anticlericalism that can be found manifested in some African American literature and even early film. And as outsiders already, Blacks have often had less to lose in openly embracing the despised identity of atheist.

When I point out the similarities between being Black and being atheistic, critics sometimes argue that the nature of racial or ethnic identity is in no way similar to a person's identity as an atheist. The two traits differ, they contend, because nature and society assign you a racial identity (you are "born with it"), whereas you choose to be an atheist. That reasoning does not reflect a true understanding of what it means to be an atheist. All persons are actually born atheists. Atheists don't choose to be such any more than they choose to accept the law of gravity. Religious persons, on the other hand, will often pick their sect in much the same manner as they choose a credit-card company or decide which auto to buy. They may be influenced by someone who reports how much they like their brand of religion, or they may decide to stick with the same variety that they grew up with. Many times they will even combine pieces from various religions that they find attractive. Faith is then used to somehow paper over contradicting realities. Atheism is, on the other hand, at its essence an uncompromising commitment to the truth. You do not choose the truth any more than you choose your race.

I had a lot of help in recognizing the truth. Ironically this assistance came in the form of the Catholic Church and its wonderful educational system.

The Catholic Church is an excellent subject for the study of Western religion in its classical form. The Catholic Church, feeling a great debt to tradition, changes only when it feels threatened. Its recognition of and response to new developments can be measured in decades, if not centuries. No doubt other religions would behave the same way, but few have such long and well-documented histories. A student of religion studies the Catholic Church as an ichthyologist learns from observing the primitive coelacanth. The Catholic Church does substantially the same things as most other Christian religions, such as establish moral standards, define doctrines of faith, and conduct various rituals. However, in its devotion to tradition Catholicism must forego any concession to modern thought. Its dogma is static and well defined, freeze-framed for easy analysis.

Beyond the virtually immutable nature of Catholic beliefs, the other main advantage to using Catholicism as a starting point in the journey to atheism is the Catholic school experience. While it might be possible to go through life without focusing on spiritual matters, not noticing the more ridiculous and inconsistent aspects of religious belief, the intensity of the Catholic school experience reduced the likelihood of such an oversight to the realm of impossibility. Education, even Jesuit education, places reason and the pursuit of knowledge at its core. The Bible says, "No man can serve two masters" (Matt. 6:24). I made reason my master. Faith had to go.

As I approach the end of my first half-century, I realize that my destiny was to be an atheist, but also that I may not have arrived at that mature state so soon had it not been for the catalyst of my religious indoctrination. How else could a rational person react to the absurdities with which a person undergoing religious training is bombarded? As a child and young man, I certainly tried to achieve the Catholic religious ideal. I went through the entire Roman Catholic regimen. After suffering under the School Sisters of Notre Dame in grade school, I was then subjected to the Society of Jesus for four years of high school, and then yet an additional three years at a Jesuit college. The term "Catholic education" came to have meaning for me on several unintended levels. The basic paradox of reason and faith was only heightened by these experiences, contrasting each against the other and sharpening my ability to distinguish them. Armed with a clear vision of the true nature of religious belief, I was better able to put the years of blind faith comfortably behind me.

Yet another advantage conferred by Catholicism, if one happens to be Black and attends Catholic school, is that you are already a minority within a minority. In most parts of the country the Catholic religion has not been particularly popular among Black people, although there are many even less-integrated sects. As a Catholic youth outside the public-school system you already feel something of the oddball. The social effects of the transition to atheism are less than they might be if you had not already been primed for it by the self-imposed segregation of Catholic school.

The transition from believer to atheist has to be more difficult if one's adult years have been invested in religious devotion. I had an easier path, having escaped religion gradually as I matured and constructed a comfortable and coherent worldview. My sense of understanding of religion was so thorough that there was no regret or sense of loss as superstition sloughed away. Neither was there any self-recrimination for my years of childlike faith. After all, at the time that I achieved apostasy, I was barely more than a child. Recognizing the truth about Jesus took only a little longer than Santa Claus. Making such a transition as an adult would have been more difficult. The cognitive dissonance alone would have been a huge impediment. How does one admit to being bamboozled by such ludicrous claims? The process would have to sound something like: "Let's see now, they told me he died and then came back to life, then floated off into heaven, and I bought it. Then they said that when I died, if I followed all the rules, I'd go to heaven, and I believed that, too. Uh, well, I was never really sure about all that. I just said I believed it to keep everybody happy." It's hardly surprising there are so few defectors. Denial is typically the primary reaction to being conned. Ironically, the more nonsensical religious belief is, the more incentive believers have to remain loyal. Who wants to admit that they were that gullible? This fear always keeps the pigeon in the con long after he or she should have admitted the truth. Then there are the social factors that weigh more heavily upon adults. How do people tell their spouses and other family members that they have stopped believing in God? Religious loyalties that destroy nations can just as easily dismember a family.

But I worked these things out in my youth even as I pursued my spiritual development in the clutches of the most ancient Christian sect. An early stage in that process was my tenure as an altar boy. Becoming an altar boy put me in some fine company: Hitler, Stalin, and Castro also brighten the ranks of former acolytes. From the perspective of an altar boy you have the opportunity to look under the skirts of the

Church and observe, to some degree, the inner workings of this institution which is presented as God's body on Earth. What did I learn? Certainly not what the Church or I expected. The first thing I noticed was that the world on the other side of the communion rail operated the same as it did everywhere else. But there was an unexpected psychological effect. The aura of sanctimony served as a lens through which everyday ironies of society were amplified, transforming the common foibles of daily life into glaring, faith-eroding absurdities.

As a fifth grader suddenly elevated to the rank of altar boy, I found myself in a position unobtainable by any of the nuns who at the time ruled a large part of my world. The balance had suddenly tilted just slightly in my favor, but only due to the peculiar and unfathomable prejudices of the Church, which gave me rank and privilege merely for having gonads that matched those of the Creator. I knew I didn't feel any holier when I put on the surplice and cassock. No Holy Spirit swooped down and made it any easier to remember those mostly meaningless Latin verses that I was supposed to mumble through the same way the priests did. But now I did things that no mere nun or any woman was permitted, even if she had taught me how to do the job. I had become the beneficiary of a discriminatory institution.

The most dramatic influences on my development were often registered by the smallest events. Goofy stuff routinely punctuated the sanctity of the Mass. What might have been passed off as normal mishaps took on added significance when they happened on the altar during Mass, only a few feet from the sanctifying graces of the Holy Eucharist, which I imagined emanated forth like some divine form of cosmic radiation. What these banal events signified, however, was not an unseen spiritual presence.

Parish priests, far from being the modern-day equivalents of the saints of old, could just as easily have been grocery clerks or basketball coaches or cab drivers. Except that they didn't work nearly as hard and were all White. Once exposed to the curious scrutiny of a fifth grader, it was soon obvious that these men of the cloth fit into the natural order of things, and by most normal measures would have to be slotted into the lower strata of that order. This fact was demonstrated in rather odd fashion one morning as I performed my duties for elderly Father Sherman. As Roland Glenn and I slogged through another boring Mass, I noticed the old priest blowing his nose. This was not unusual, and most priests kept a handkerchief tucked away somewhere for that purpose, a necessary concession to human imperfection. After stuffing his handkerchief back into his sleeve, Father Sherman turned to face the congregation. There, dangling from the very tip of his huge, ancient, hooked nose was a long, disgusting booger. This repellant mass, swinging back and forth, resembled some poor groundcrewman swept up on the end of the Hindenberg's mooring rope. Oh, the humanity! Totally oblivious to his absurd appearance, the celebrant of this most sacred of Catholic rituals boomed the familiar, ancient words of benediction, "Dominus vobiscum." As the long thread of mucus danced in front of his mouth, my eyes were drawn to it until it seemed to jump out at me, like a special effect in some vulgar 3-D movie. My words of response, "Et cum spiritu tuo," took on a distinctly ironic connotation at that point, and I was forced to once again confront the incongruity between these sometimes wildly unsanctified events and the "special relationship with God" that this holy sacrament was supposed to help confer. Forget the problem of the existence of evil, or God's failure to relieve the suffering of innocents. Why did he permit that booger to swing on the tip of Father Sherman's nose? The thought of what might have happened when this doddering old priest moved the consecrated host to his mouth was a direct affront to the sanctity of the Eucharist. Supposedly this unleavened bread was transformed into the body of Christ. I couldn't tell by looking. But I could tell that the man who was in the process of performing this miracle had a booger hanging from his nose.

I was fortunate that my religious experience was gained in the Catholic Church. Other, less formalized, less authoritarian, less White religions might not have offered such a starkly well-defined analog for society's absurdity and injustice. Religion was of course simply one aspect of reality that turned out to be completely different from what it first seemed. Another big discovery that paralleled this process of demystification was the sorting out of racial issues. Religious beliefs, with their emphasis on "chosen people," substitutive redemption, and other concepts which focused on heritage and identity, began to resemble the racist beliefs so much in debate in the 1960s; they were merely different types of "faith." The solution to these problems seemed obvious: reason.

Given an open mind, faith yields to knowledge, and I got plenty of knowledge about race and religion at Catholic school. Most of my fellow students at parochial school were White, even after the local public school had become 90 percent Black. It seemed as if the remaining White students were taking refuge there. Unable to join the other Whites in flight to the suburbs, these stragglers, always of limited financial resources, were a skewed representation of the White population, making it even easier to eradicate any thoughts of inferiority which I might have picked up from society at large. The implied inferiority of Black people on television and the subtle racism of the Sisters of Notre Dame hardly stacked up with my own experience with White classmates who were the children of the bottom rungs of the White working class. These kids were obviously no better off, and no better, than we were. Even at that age I recognized that Catholic school, in exchange for the meager patronage received from these hardscrabble parents, offered a refuge from the sometimes cruel realities of public school. Likewise, religion created a false world to shelter believers from the rest of reality.

Impecunious White students were not alone in finding sanctuary in parochial schools. Even the janitors were like characters in some Fellini movie. But the nuns and priests were the most enigmatic. Much youthful speculation was directed toward the true nature of nuns, and how they related to other women. It was obvious that they repressed the normal displays of femininity, but to precisely what length this masking was carried provided endless grist for boyish conjecture. Once, while helping move supplies in the convent, I noticed a huge case of Kotex, a sight which I found for some reason surprising. Certainly these were women, but the apparent denial of their femininity seemed unnatural and somehow even perverse. Despite such attempts to circumvent what most people consider natural, it was readily apparent to us children that, no matter how weird, nuns and priests held no special place in the order of things. In fact, in their cloistered existence, so apparently naïve in the eyes of us streetwise youth, they could easily be seen as fragile and even impotent in the real world. This impression was dramatized when we drove our sixth-grade teacher, Sister Imelda, from her classroom in the middle of the term. She had to be bundled off to wherever they take nuns who have lost their grip. If her religious devotion, with all its asceticism, couldn't spare her from the mild antics of a fairly normal group of eleven- and twelve-year-olds, of what use was it?

Catholicism is all about authority. You believe the specific things such as transubstantiation and the virgin birth because you are told to, not as the result of any logical process. Atheism, on the other hand, came to me as an almost natural process. Nobody told me to believe anything, or even said I should become a freethinker. In contrast, Catholicism provided a highly defined concept of faith and religious authority, training me for years about these things in both academic and real-life applications. Since the whole system is based upon faith rather than reason, the authority is necessarily absolute and unquestioning. There is little point in debating mysteries. This does not distinguish Catholicism from other religions, but Catholicism is particularly unabashed about the role of authority in faith. Yet what I experienced in my religious life could only lead me to question Catholic authority. The transition from questioning a supposedly divinely inspired authority to questioning God was but a short one, because what is a personal, omniscient, omnipotent God if not the ultimate authority? And if I found myself unable to accept the authority of the Catholic Church, how could I accept its teachings? Moreover, perhaps more to the point, if I could not accept the authority of a flawed but at least obviously extant Church, how could I bend my knee to something which, after all was said and done, could not be proven to be anything more than a motley collection of hand-me-down myths and deliberately fabricated propaganda? I realized that such things were about all any religion offered.

As an atheist my only possible regret is that now I have to face reality in its entirety, with no benevolent spirits to explain away the rough spots. It is easy, in a particularly dark moment, to envy the bliss that comes with embracing a fantasy. Ironically, one of the harshest realities is the damage inflicted on humanity by the various faiths. The constant burden that religious thought imposes upon our societies is truly staggering. The ugly side effects of religion manifest themselves daily in hatred and violence, ignorance and superstition. Admittedly religion has been far from the only source of strife, but it has without question been a leading contributor. Religion has motivated chari-table deeds, but all too often these apparent good works have been used as weapons in the competition among faiths. As I write this, hundreds of people are dying in religious violence in Indonesia, the latest of many hot spots. I sometimes fear for humanity's future when I think of the deadly potential of religious devotion.

12.

MY LONG AND WINDING ROAD TO HUMANISM

Nkeonye Otakpor

I was born in a rural community of subsistence farmers and petty traders. I grew up in the bosom of my four grandparents on both sides—paternal and maternal. I also met the elder brother of my paternal grandfather.

My grandparents (paternal and maternal) were well-known and established traditional doctors, medicine men and women. They were neither kings nor chiefs, but were wealthy by the standards of their time. None of them ever went to church. Yet they believed in God and practiced the religion of their Igbo tribe—the kind of religion now known as Traditional African Religion.

My father was not schooled in the Western European lifestyle, but he had an English name. It was fashionable to have an English name during his time. He never went to church. He believed in the Igbo god and practiced Igbo religion.

My mother went to church at an early age, where she was baptized with an English name. Upon marrying my father, she kept her English name, but stopped attending church services. Rather, she reverted to the Igbo god and religion. Upon the death of my father, she returned to the church.

Before I was born, my mother had given birth to ten other children. None was alive when I was born. I am the eleventh child and an only son. My sister is the twelfth. Only two of us out of the twelve are here in this interesting, sunlit, difficult but fascinating world.

At home, I was taught to put others before self, and to consider the needs of others before mine. I was taught by my grandparents that the needs of others are more important than those of self. These were not mere platitudes, because these sentiments were often given practical effects.

Our home was consequently an abode for anyone in need of shelter and food, or any kind of assistance. They often went out of their way to help others in need. These others were often not blood relations. Occasionally, they were complete strangers who came along soliciting for one form of assistance or the other.

This view is morally defensible against the background of Igbo ethics, which emphasizes the brotherhood of all human beings. According to the Igbo, the entire human race is one whole family: *ANYI BU OFU*. Second, it is morally grounded in the Igbo idea of a man being his brother's keeper, because it has been proven that when the nose is affected or afflicted, the eyes weep. Our tradition as taught by our ancestors insists that we share whatever is available.

This is possible because, among the Igbo, there are no cousins, nephews, nieces, aunts, and uncles. Every male relation is a brother and every female relation is a sister. In Igbo culture—like most Africans—the sons and daughters of aunts and uncles are simply brothers and sisters, not cousins.

With any brothers and sisters, and occasionally some "strange faces," we ate food in the open courtyard where it was served. There is not a special invitation to breakfast, lunch, or dinner. Anyone in the household during mealtime who is hungry has a right to eat. Passersby are free to eat without invitation. It is morally repugnant

not to eat with friends, neighbors, and relations. It is morally repre-
hensible for one who is known to be hungry to refuse to eat when
food is served. Such refusal may be interpreted as an act of bad faith.

My parents, grandparents, and other adult relations all prayed to
the Igbo god at dawn and at sunset. They prayed for good harvest.
They prayed for rain during acute periods of drought. They prayed to
avert famine and disease. They prayed before and after meals. They
prayed for a good life while also praying for the prevention of evil in
their lives. I was therefore nurtured in an environment that was
deeply religious but not altogether irrational.

The first achievement of the English colonial administrators (at
least on the psychological plane, which is not insignificant) was the
radical displacement and substitution of the Igbo god with the European god. New prayers and supplications were taught and directed to
the new god.

I am the first grandchild allowed the full benefit of Western education in my family. Other members before me, for various reasons,
particularly opposition from my grandparents, never had this full benefit. They stopped halfway through primary school.

My grandparents reasoned that the "freeborn" were not to go to
school to avoid a situation where they will mix with the Europeans.
The "slaves," servants, and ne'er-do-wells were those allowed to mix
with the Europeans. They were the ones allowed to go to school.
Thus, they were the early converts to Christianity.

I was allowed to go to school due mainly to my stubborn dispo-
sition as a child. At an early age I rejected the farm, ran home often
from the farm, and accompanied my mother to the market. It was in
an attempt to find something worthwhile to occupy me and curb my
stubbornness that my grandparents let me go to school, though
grudgingly. Moreover, everything was done to please my sister and
me—but particularly me—so that we could stay put in this world.
This was understandable against the background of the psychological
trauma my mother had been through before I was born.

Upon entering the primary school, I was easily identified by the
instructor who taught me catechism. I was baptized and confirmed
early enough because of my activities in the school (which increased

in the church) as the need arose. I began as a class monitor and soon became the school prefect. I became an altar boy before I finished my primary education.

Therefore, at a very early age I had the privilege of working closely with catechists and priests. Working as an altar boy enabled me—occasionally—to be part of the priest's household.

My activities as an altar boy followed me to the teacher's training college where I spent two years. During that period, I was the most visible altar boy, because I had done it so long.

I was employed as a student teacher after my training. In that capacity, my involvement in religious activities blossomed. In addition to my primary assignment, I was an auxiliary catechist. I taught my pupils catechism and prepared them for baptism and the sacrament of confirmation. I continued assisting the priests in the sacristy and, on important occasions, assisted in the celebration of mass—the "holy communion."

I was twenty-four when the first military coup took place in Nigeria in January 1966. This was followed by the countercoup, both of which presaged the civil war. The war did two things to me simultaneously. First, the futility of prayers became evident for the first time ever. All the prayers said to prevent the war came to naught. The prayers did not save close relatives and countless others who died during the crisis. Second, it showed that only human beings can prevent war, its agony and catastrophe, simply because wars are the result of human failings. War (including those fought in the name of God) exemplifies the ease with which mankind descends into barbarism. Both sides of the conflict prayed to the same God for success and for assistance in the killings before and during the war. Against the background of the number of people who were killed during the period it is obvious that God heard the prayers from both sides. Not only did God hear their prayers, their requests were granted, and in full.

The trauma of the war, the agony, the suffering, the hardship, and the unbelievable show of wickedness and inhumanity led me to my first statement in which I expressed doubts concerning the existence of God.

Without knowing anything about secularism or humanism I argued, to the surprise of friends, that no God exists. I argued then, as I do now, that if God existed he must be unjust to simply sit back and watch humanity butcher itself. Children, the aged, pregnant women, and others, were systematically murdered merely for the fun of it, or simply because they did not belong to the right tribe.

It was impossible for me to argue beyond the limits of my knowledge. But on the basis of what happened during that war which I witnessed, I was no longer comfortable with the idea of a just, good God, up there in the heavens, listening to prayers, and providing solutions to sundry human problems. During that war, God was methodically absent, as is always the case. God was not interested in what humanity did to itself and their reasons for doing so.

At the end of the war, life gradually returned to normal. I resumed my teaching career. Lacking a strong financial base from which to draw in support of further studies, I started reading at home. I ordered correspondence-course materials from Welsey Hall, Oxford University. With these course materials, I prepared for the General Certificate of Education (G.C.E.) examinations conducted by the University of London.

Two things happened then. First, in order to achieve my aim, I had to relocate to the nearest township, so that I could avail myself of a public library. Second, I was able to buy newspapers. Consequently I encountered the writings of the irrepressible and extravagantly humane educationist and columnist, the late Tai Solarin. His column titled "Thinking With You," which appeared every Thursday on the pages of the *Daily Times* newspaper, was an eye-opener. It was as if he were writing the column only for me. I read it all.

It was from this column that I was finally able to find fulfillment in terms of my doubt concerning the existence of God. Tai Solarin presented arguments to the effect that God does not exist. He was convincing enough. The rest, as they say, is history.

Tai Solarin was energetic and resourceful. He quoted often from the works of Bertrand Russell and H. G. Wells. I could not read H. G. Wells until I got to Europe. In the public library I was happy to find Russell's *Why I Am Not a Christian*.

After reading Russell, in addition to the weekly column maintained by Solarin, my attendance at religious services gradually declined. By the time I went to Europe to further my education, I had stopped going to church services.

During the same period, as I was settling down in my new location, a male teacher impregnated his girlfriend, a female teacher in the primary school where I also taught. The reaction of the church was swift. Both were dismissed from the teaching service of the Catholic mission, owners of the primary school. Their offense was that they had sex before marriage, that is to say fornication, which was then regarded as a mortal sin against God and man. The fact that they decided to get married did not save their jobs. It meant nothing to the church.

I did not understand what God had to do with sex. In any case, I joined other staff in appealing on their behalf. The appeals and petitions achieved nothing.

Interestingly, at the same time in another parish adjacent to our own, an Irish reverend gentleman and parish priest was caught by his parishioners having sex with the wife of the catechist. The punishment he got was simple: he was returned to his native Ireland. He was not dismissed from the service of the church.

This double standard was understood and was resisted in the form of work stoppages, which filtered out as the church authorities ingeniously managed the crisis. The message was not lost. The idea of one God for the European and the Igbo was under threat. I questioned the idea innocently.

This was the situation when I went to Europe in 1973 to further my education. In Europe I experienced culture shock in its most severe form. I was lonely, indeed, very lonely. It was a very bad situation coming straight from a culture where loneliness is virtually unknown. With no one to talk to, and fearful of being arrested and deported for walking the streets, I became a prisoner in my room with my TV, radio, pipe and tobacco as my companions. I loved the latter duo.

To make matters exceedingly difficult, I was a private student. I had to work in order to finance my education, pay my bills, and maintain myself as a young man.

I experienced what it means to be Black, to be an African. Very few people would sit near me in a bus or train. Those who did, did so reluctantly and were careful not to allow our bodies to touch. Consequently, I was frustrated, friendless, psychologically low, and angry for ever leaving my home, my village, my relations and friends, and my country. On several occasions I thought of returning to Nigeria, only to discard the idea.

Against this background, I nursed the idea of going back to church services on a number of occasions. The more I tried not to, the more the thought persisted. By this time I had completed two years of my undergraduate work. I was happy that I was able to continue schooling, but unhappy with my economic situation.

Then one Sunday morning in late summer, I went to church services in one of the most Catholic countries in Europe, if not the entire world.

My second shocking experience was that I found only old men and women, and the very young—boys and girls—in the church. The same pattern was replicated on subsequent occasions.

My third shock was that nobody would sit near me inside the church. I found my experiences in the buses, trains, and trams replicated inside a church which is regarded as the house of God. I was more than surprised. I was numbed. I felt humiliated. I felt outside myself and the world. I felt betrayed by the Catholic church, its colonial officials in Nigeria, and its doctrine. I felt betrayed by the neo-colonial purveyors of the church dogma in Nigeria and elsewhere.

It was clear to me that the church was not the house of God where the equality of all men and women has been loudly proclaimed. I found that it is illusory to think of human equality even inside a church. I had returned to religious services in order to seek comfort, but I had found only more discomfort and agony in the process. I stopped attending church services. I have not done so since 1975. I will never do so again. I do not consider myself a religious person, whatever that means. I am absolutely unchurched.

Interestingly, beginning from my second year in the university, the following courses were mounted in the faculty: philosophy of religion, psychology of religion, and sociology of religion. I took an unusual interest in these courses, because they assisted me in finding some answers to the religious issues that bothered me. In addition, I read the works of Ludwig Feuerbach, Nietzsche, and other philosophers. I completed my intellectual journey into atheism when I was taught Marxism. After reading Marx and his acolytes I concluded on the basis of my experiences and readings that there is no God. None ever existed.

Religion is an ideology. In the context of the ideology of imperialism and colonialism, it was an essential aspect of the armor with which non-Europeans were subjugated and humiliated. In many parts of the world religion is still being employed to play the same role, unfortunately, by the indigenous peoples.

Yet religion has a social function as well as a psychological one. It is one of the social institutions. But it is wishful thinking to ascribe any other functions to religion or its symbols. This is a human world and the religious instinct as a social product is part of it. It is neither a divine world nor God's world.

God, if ever it existed, never had any business in this world. All the assistance I had during my study years in Europe was from fellow humans who empathized with my condition. There were those who shared with me, showed solidarity, took me into their homes for lunch or dinner, and assisted me in getting employment during summer. In all these episodes and more, God was not there, implicitly or explicitly.

I returned to Nigeria at the completion of my studies to find that one of my paternal brothers, an invalid from birth, had been excommunicated from the Catholic church. The reason was that he defaulted in the payment of church dues. I was not shocked anymore. The church is supposed to support invalids, but an invalid was driven away from the church simply because he was unable to support the church, financially and materially. He could not because he was physically disabled from birth.

My faith in atheism was further strengthened by that development. This faith took the direction of no return when in the late 1980s I sent an essay to *Free Inquiry* for assessment and possible publication. In addition, I requested a sample copy because I had known nothing about the journal. The essay was not published but the sample copy was sent. Ever since, *Free Inquiry* has become my bible.

With this journal I successfully crossed the Rubicon. There are no regrets because there is no reason for any. There is no going back because there is no reason for that.

It has been easy for me to substitute the garb of humanism for that of religion because of (a) the influence of my parents and grandparents, and (b) the fact that there are aspects of humanism in Igbo ethics, politics, and the way of life.

In the political sphere decisions are taken in the assembly of all adult citizens. It is an assembly where no one is denied free speech in the process of deliberation and decision making. In ethics there is emphasis on tolerance, accommodation, and mutuality. The live-and-let-live principle is held in high esteem.

Now, how can humanism benefit humanity? I have learned over the years that service to humanity is most fulfilling, satisfying, and enduring. The more so if such a service is selfless, as it should be.

Fortunately, humanity has no reference point outside itself. Humanity is its own reference point. Humanism can benefit humanity by suggesting to all those who subscribe to *The Affirmations of Humanism—A Statement of Principles* to endeavor to make these principles their own articles of faith.[1] These are lofty principles that can be actualized by all of us. The actualization of these principles can help in the cocreation of new values and history, and in that process, remake our world.

NOTE

1. *Editor's note: The Affirmations of Humanism* are values based on science, reason, and democracy. They provide a secular alternative to traditional religion, and serve as a rational and ethical guide for living. They are authored by Paul Kurtz, the founder of Prometheus Books and the Council for Secular Humanism, and are available at the Council.

13.

HOW I BECAME AN ATHEIST

Gebregeorgis Yohannes

I was born and raised in the nomadic Borana region of Southern Ethiopia. My father was a peasant from northern Ethiopia. He left his village when he was very young, and I remember the story he told me of how he left the village. As a young boy my father went to the village priest to study. The only schools then were church schools. Young boys were assigned to a particular priest and studied under him for many years. The priest my father was studying under was blind. He made his students do all kinds of hard work in his home and on his farm. Students also shared the responsibility of guiding him wherever he went. The students were like indentured servants to the priest, who also treated them very harshly. One day it was my father's turn to lead the priest, and instead of leading him on a clear path, he took him into a thorny bush and left him there. My father was tired of the abuse he was receiving from his priest-teacher. Very soon my father left the village, headed south, and landed in Negelle, where I was born. My father enrolled me at the government school in Negelle when I turned six. Negelle was a small town with people of different ethnic origins and beliefs, mostly Christians and Muslims. The school, however, had more Orthodox Christian children such as myself. The Orthodox Church was the dominant religion in Ethiopia. It was the state religion, and the king claimed to be the "elect of God," with full approval of the church. I was in fourth grade and only twelve years old. One of the classes we had was called "gibregebinet" (morals). A priest by the name of Girma taught this class throughout the school, but only for Orthodox children. We called him "awraris," or rhinoceros, because of his protruding front teeth. Whenever he came to class, the first thing he said was "Tsau dekikene Islam," which means "Children of Islam go out." The Muslim kids would bolt out of the class as soon as he uttered the words. Sometimes he would lash at their running bottoms for no reason. As soon as they had left, he would turn to us and punish us severely for every trifling reason. The most serious punishment awaited any child who had not gone to church on Sundays. He assigned students and everyone had to register with him. His punishments ranged from constant whipping to making us kneel down on a concrete floor with tiny gravel under our knees. On top of that we had to stretch both our arms to shoulder level. If we slacked our hands, he would come and whip the hands. He also had a bunch of rusty keys with which he would knock our heads. In fact, one day he had knocked one child called Haile on his head so hard that blood spurted out of his head like a fountain. Every child lived in fear of awraris and nobody could free us from his tyranny. Corporal punishment is acceptable in schools, and teachers punish their students any way they see fit. In fact, corporal punishment is the norm everywhere with varying degrees of severity. Awraris's punishment was the most cruel compared to all other teachers' punishment. As far as teaching us morals, God only knows if we learned any, except fear.

The Muslim children had all the fun in their morals class. Their teacher—whom the Muslim children lovingly call Hajji (one who has made the pilgrimage to Mecca)—was a very kind and adorable person. He told his children tales of his own adventures and other fantastic tales and songs. He occasionally treated his children with "halawas" (candy) and pastries, which his wife made. At times Hajji would even give us some whenever he had some left over. Oh, how we Christian urchins envied our Muslim counterparts! They were the happiest children, while we were mostly miserable.

My relationship to the priesthood changed very drastically way back. During the many religious holidays, priests would go from house to house to sprinkle the holy water, to let people "kiss the meskel," and to eat and drink. Meskel is a cross, and all priests carry a small hand-cross around wherever they go (sometimes wrapped in a piece of cloth). It's customary for Orthodox Christians to bow their heads whenever and wherever they encounter a priest and to kiss the cross. The priest will raise it up to the forehead of the person and move it across the face.

Whenever a priest came to our house I would bolt and disappear to avoid being sprinkled with water and to avoid kissing the cross. On the street, when our parents or relatives would see a priest they would stop and kiss the cross. But I would always stand far away. My parents thought that I would do this because I was shy, which I was, but that was not the reason I kept a distance from the priests. That was my way of rebelling.

After I finished eighth grade, I had to attend high school 375 kilometers away—north to Yirgalem in the southern province of Sidamo. There was only one high school in the whole province. As in elementary school, there was also a mandatory morals class in high school. But due to a relatively small number of Muslims coming to high school, there was only an Orthodox Christian morals class. On the first day of morals class, the teacher asked if there were any Muslims in the class. I raised my hand very quickly. He asked me my name. I told him my name, which is typically Christian, both first and last. He asked how I could be a Muslim and have a Christian name. I told him that I had converted to Islam. I was lying, but I was saved the ordeal of sitting in a moralless morals class. As far as becoming a Muslim, I used to say that if I needed a religion, I'd be a Muslim. Of course, this was at the beginning of my doubt about Christianity, and before I was able to explore what Islam really was. I have always said that almost everyone has a terrible experience with these ignorant morals teachers throughout the country, save maybe a handful. They were the most cruel—at times psychotic—individuals. This was a very crucial beginning of my rebellion and hatred for religious beliefs, save the traditional animistic or natural religions such as what the Boranases of my childhood believed in. It's much better, I believed, to worship nature because you can see and feel its power, its destructiveness, and its benevolence. These beliefs make much more sense than the pie-in-the-sky, you'll-go-to-hell-or-heaven beliefs which are ridiculous and which are based on childlike fears. As my disbelief in God increased, so did my realization of how millions of Ethiopians were cheated into perpetual poverty by attributing every calamity to an act of God. According to the belief of most Ethiopians, God writes everyone's fate. Only *he* has the power to make someone poor, sickly, and miserable. Most Ethiopians believe in the afterlife and eagerly await the day they will go to heaven. Most of the Ethiopian priesthood is illiterate, even when it comes to the belief itself. Most priests have a rudimentary knowledge of the so-called word of God, which is a sorry compilation of folklore and fiction. Most of the priests are peasants who took the vow to live a parasitic life over other peasants. Most of our parents never knew what is written in the Bible. Church services are rendered in an almost-dead church language called Geez, which even most priests do not know unless they have memorized it by rote. The priesthood lives off the poor peasant farmer in a constant holiday feast in commemoration of a myriad saints who are not even in the Book. Ethiopians spend half their lives not doing any work, as every day of the month is a saint's day. In fact, there are more saints than the number of days in a month.

It's no wonder that Ethiopia is one of the poorest countries in the world and is known for poverty, disease, death, destruction, and human misery. "Ethiopia has stretched her hands unto God" for far too long. Unless this stretching of hands to a God who does not help stops, religions and superstitions will forever enslave Ethiopians. Ethiopians have to turn to themselves as sources of life and liberty, and do everything in their own power to change the dire circumstances they are in. To add insult to injury, Ethiopia is also a fertile ground for all kinds of evangelism. Wherever there is abject poverty and ignorance, there is a market for religious conversion. There are now Mormons, Moonies, Pentecostals, Jehovah's Witnesses, Bahais, and lots of other religious sects having a feast converting people to their respective cults. This is in addition to the traditional beliefs of Orthodox Christianity and Islam, which have long roots in Ethiopia, and the Western churches such as the Adventists, Protestants, Catholics, and the like.

Most Ethiopians, young and old alike, have given up on the prospects of their worldly life changing and are easily willing to be taken by any religious cult that promises them an unknown happy future and which can at the same time give them some money, clothing, and food. Most cults come from the West loaded with money. The Moonies are spending millions of birr to convert young university students. They work in secrecy and with high-sounding names such as "Women's Federation for World Peace." The Mormons are also in the works. These new cults are infecting the minds of young people with their pie-in-the-sky and reward in the afterworld nonsense. Young students are married to people they have never met and shipped off to Korea—the Holy Land of Moonies—to labor in factories. The money is collected by their "holy parent," Reverend Moon. His children have no need for money as long as he has bank accounts in his name for them.

If one can change religious beliefs as one does his shirts, then it doesn't make any sense to have faith in the first place. Many people hop from one religion to another, but one is no better than the next. They are all fabrications of the human imagination. People, as we know, have created thousands of gods, angels, fairies, monsters, devils, and all kinds of fictional characters for centuries. There will still be more to come. Humanity, unless it is liberated from the shackles of religious tyranny and fear, will not reach its full potential.

As a young man, even though I couldn't believe in any of the fairy tales of religion, I had lingering fears of offending others, of being alienated, of retribution, and of the wrath of a society which is blinded by faith. For many years I pretended to be a believer and paid lip service to a God I never had any use for. But some three or four years back, after over thirty years of internal struggle, I convinced myself that I would not live in fear anymore. I created the motto "the beginning of wisdom is to do away with fear," and since then, I have not shied away from speaking my mind about my disbelief in God or any of the superstitions attached to it. In fact, I'm convinced that the only way we can liberate people and societies is if we can liberate them from the shackles of religion and superstition.

14.

SALVATION THROUGH EDUCATION

Dominic I. Ogbonna

Looking at my childhood one would have thought that I was carefully cut out to be a priest. Though the youngest member of my village Block Rosary Crusade, I enjoyed its executive membership. I led church services, composed pious songs, upbraided "sinners," won awards for catechetical literacy, and saw winged angels in the sky each time lightning appeared.

When my father sent me to the junior seminary for my secondary education, though, I didn't know what it was all about. (He told me he was sending me to a place where I would receive "great education.") Finding out was not difficult, however, for our seminary training was generously religious: formal prayers four times daily, with intermittent bells reminding us of the angels; prayers before and after each lesson and meal; innumerable spiritual conferences, retreats, and the like, all interspersed with occasional sessions with the bishop, who spoke unceasingly of Saints Theresa and Dominic Saviour. Even the pope could not have hoped for a better religious education.

Not that this kind of education helped much. Our seminary had more than its fair share of the crudities which characterized secondary education in Nigeria in those days. Let me give you a few examples. The senior student who occupied the bed below mine (the bed was a double bunk, and I occupied the top position) not infrequently made me sleep on the bare wet floor under his bed, and this punitive action was by no means peculiar.

In 1982 a student stole out at night and permanently disfigured the face of his sleeping teacher with a concentrated acid solution! Barely four years later in the same school, several students stole school property.

Of course, such scandalous cases are carefully concealed from the public (who would rather believe that the seminary houses angels, an image zealously guarded by the authorities). But such cases would provide food for thought for those who believe that religious training is the best way to produce decent citizens. I have carefully studied the late Dr. Tai Solarin's Mayflower School (the only secular school in Nigeria, which was run by an outspoken atheist), and I do not think that our seminarians could have competed with Tai's students in either moral virtue or academic excellence.

After my college education in the junior seminary, I proceeded to the senior seminary to study philosophy. The religious life of the senior seminary differs from its junior counterpart only in being more exaggerated and hypocritical. In my first year I read Kant's *Critique of Pure Reason*, and although I didn't understand what he was talking about, I got this much: that *space* and *time* are necessary conditions for any valid knowledge. God and his spirits were obviously not in spatiotemporal relations. I began wondering whether we really knew anything about them.

The real blows to my faith, however, came during my second year. Three books particularly got me thinking. The first was Morton Prince's *Dissociation of Personality*, a most interesting study in abnormal psychology. Prince's book not only challenged my ideas about the soul, but introduced me to modern psychology. The second was Bertrand Russell's *Skeptical Essays* where, to my utmost amazement, I found many ideas which I had suppressed, believing them to be devilish. Was I thrilled! I subsequently read Russell's works with such regularity that some students started regarding me as a communist plant. The third book was Darwin's *Origin of Species,* first recommended to me by my brilliant lecturer in philosophical anthropology, who had taught courses on biological evolution and cosmogenesis.

These books and many others introduced me to the world of modern science; and it didn't require much reading on my part to realize that most of the metaphysical and moral opinions I had been brought up to believe under the cloak of sacred religion were either palpably false or uncertain.

I suppose the average American knows about the big bang. But there are graduate students in Nigeria who have never heard of and will never hear about the big bang, and they are not in the minority. That is the way it is in Nigeria. Imagine, then, how surprised I was to learn that the creation story in Genesis, for instance, is an ancient and unoriginal tale as good (or as bad) as the ones we tell under moonlight in my village. Gradually I started losing my religious faith.

Of course, losing my religious faith was anything but funny. I simply did not want to lose it. For one thing, I had been in the seminary for so long and had grown so used to its ways that I could hardly imagine myself living any life outside the priesthood. For another, the socioeconomic conditions in Nigeria have been in an awful mess, and the priesthood is one very peculiar profession, where economic security and social status are generously guaranteed. For a third (and perhaps most important) reason, loss of faith in a person with as religious an upbringing as mine could also result in a loss of existential meaning. (I am happy to have gotten over the emotional crises and their consequent suicidal temptations which initially followed my loss of faith.)

Because of these problems I was deathly afraid of losing my faith, and therefore fought valiantly to preserve it. I cried hysterically to God and begged him to save the faith in him that I was rapidly losing.

I devised special prayers and novenas, and even undertook some chastening rituals to achieve this same end. But either the deity was not there, or he was enjoying some deep slumber punctuated with sweet romantic dreams. My prayers, so far as I could see, were not answered, because I continued to lose my faith.

In any event, books were available. I was sure that by reading about this universe, I would find some unshakable truth on which my faith could be anchored. So I voraciously read literature ranging from philosophy to psychology, anthropology, geology, astronomy (thanks, Carl Sagan, your *Cosmos* moved me, and I have since read it thrice), physiology, physics, psychic research—just name it. The more I read, however, the more I found additional reasons for the same conclusion. I told myself, "Stop begging poor God to restore your faith, man. It was a big mistake to have had faith in the first place." When I finally read some texts on Scripture and comparative religion, the line was drawn for me. For once, I clearly saw the priesthood for what it was: a hypocritical lifestyle; a recidivist anachronism perpetuated to serve itself by exploiting the hopes of those who still allow themselves to be intimidated by the fears inherited from the infancy of the human race. Obviously the priesthood was not for me. I decided to leave.

It must not be thought that my situation was unusual. There are seminarians who really believe Christian hogwash, and whose priestly zeal equals that of the missionaries. Such seminarians, however, are exceptionally rare, and are outstanding in the seminary environment, where they cut the image of an ancient species threatened with extinction. In their private lives, the majority of the modern priests and seminarians in Nigeria either know and accept Christianity for the hogwash it is, or believe a sanitized version of it which would certainly scandalize the wits out of ordinary believers. I knew a student who, instead of swallowing the communion wafers he received at mass, painstakingly made a collection of the lot which he dutifully flushed down the toilet at the end of each week, with a grin on his face. Another had sex with a woman inside a church.

Nigeria has the most heavily populated seminary in the world, and a rapidly expanding priestly population. Church authorities call this a vocation boom, and interpret it as a sign that the Christian deity will rechristen Europe through Africa (shout "hosanna!" ye Africans!). Well, I am not in a position to know what games the deity might have decided to play with Africa. What I do know for sure is that, for most modern priests and seminarians in Nigeria, the priesthood is not so much a means of saving the soul as a way to support the body. In a depressed and grossly corrupt economy, the priesthood is regarded as (and is) one of the easiest ways of climbing the social ladder and achieving economic security. Even the Vatican has begun to realize this fact. (In 1987, the papal pro nuncio in Nigeria sent a letter to the rectors of the major seminaries, warning that the Nigerian vocation was becoming "dubious." He admitted this much because he never loved Nigeria.)

Of course, secular humanists should not take solace in this development. Whether or not Nigerian priests believe the doctrine, they certainly work to promote it, if only because it serves their interests. Rome and other Western religious powers are using their imposing financial powers to ensure that Africa carries Christianity into the twenty-first century, a task rendered easy by the poverty and illiteracy which currently plague the continent. (In 1986 the pope said, "The future hope of the church lies in Africa and South America. Europe is tired.")

The religious indoctrination of the continent is much worse than the ideological and economic devastation which followed the colonial experience. For while an African can easily abandon his native gods when confronted with science (our traditional religions significantly lack dogmatism), the African Christian would find it very difficult to abandon Jesus. Put simply, the ongoing religious brainwashing ensures that in the twenty-first century Africa will have to fight the intellectual wars of the Enlightenment. Thanks, church.

There is much more to say about the factors which promote the religious vocations in Nigeria, but let me just mention the role played by public opinion. When I left the seminary, I was practically ostracized from my village and from many other social circles. People saw me and pretended I was not there. Former friends turned enemies. A rumor started by my uncle (a clergyman) that I was insane became widely believed. The pressure became so great that my parents had to change their residence. (The experience was very traumatic for them.

Today my home is as hot for me as the quantum phase of the big bang, simply because I do not go to church. I have to avoid going home as much as possible to avoid quarreling with my parents, who have never heard of Darwin. They have heard of Elijah a million times, though.) My agnosticism has cost me a job here and there, but with few exceptions I find it all to be quite humorous.

I eventually visited the late secular humanist Dr. Tai Solarin, who not only was kind to me, but also helped sponsor my education. And today I no longer think I still need to work for the deity or be in the Jesus enterprise.

15.

REBEL WITH A CAUSE

Micah Lamptey

My twin brother and I were born on September 3, 1966, in Tema, Ghana. I can still remember when we were baptized into the Presbyterian Church at the age of six. We were Christened Micah and Michael.

We attended the Traditional Elementary School, and there was a Sunday school in our neighborhood. My brother and I loved attending the Sunday school very much. We were very punctual; we did not want to miss the Bible stories, especially those about Elijah and Elisha, Daniel and the lion's den, and those about Meschach, Shadrach, and Abednego. We took part in the National Sunday School Quiz contests and won many prizes, including Bibles.

Some years later, I can remember my mother diligently persuading us to take the confirmation classes, and we were later confirmed at the same Presbyterian church. We were then issued red cards that made us eligible to attend the Lord's Supper.

But when I was about eighteen years old, I attended a technical institution, studying automotive engineering. I started facing difficulties in life because our father was neglecting us. There was a Scripture Union (SU) on campus, and after my girlfriend invited me to join, I became a member.

Whenever I attended the meetings I could answer all the biblical questions that were posed to me. But I realized that there was a degree of emotionalism or spirituality in the members' behavior that was lacking in me. I didn't want to fake it and say, "I'm also spiritual," so I waited for the "holy spirit" to take absolute control of me. But though I prayed incessantly, nothing happened.

By the time I had completed technical school, our father's neglect had spawned so many difficulties for me that I decided to increase my faith in God, hoping things would work out better. Our mother even led us to a churchwoman who asked us to fast and pray. But as unpleasant as the fasting was, I didn't even get what I prayed for.

I continued my education at Polytechnic, and one day I decided to go to church—a Baptist church. I realized that the larger portion of what the preacher said consisted of pure lies. It didn't apply to real-life situations, and I didn't feel that I would be losing anything if I never went to church again—and I haven't been back since.

I started reading the Bible to see if I was missing something in the Holy Book. But I felt insulted by a passage from Paul that said it was due to the fact that the Jews refused to accept the Lord and his message that the message is now being brought to the Gentiles. Paul went on to say that the situation may be likened to that of a tree whose branch has been cut off. The branch of another tree is being substituted at that joint. The tree would not be like the original (it would be imperfect), and the Gentiles would not forget this. We are all waiting for the day when the Jews accept the Lord and his message. How could Almighty God favor some of his children over others?

I also wondered how science had surpassed religion and brought improved living conditions to humanity, yet Christians and other religionists condemned science and propagated their faiths. One day I became furious thinking about how I had dedicated my life to God without him listening to me. I took out the red confirmation card and burned it, and I wasn't exactly happy with my mother for having given me the card in the first place. Now, when faced with a problem, I have found no other way to solve it than through reason.

From an early age I had loved being good to human beings, because I realized that life could be extremely tough for some people. And I am still willing to help whenever I can. But I found it absurd that religions, which profess goodwill to humankind, incite and propagate violence, war, and murder, and say that we humans are worthless in the sight of God. Moreover, they contend that we are living only due to his grace. I didn't need that kind of grace.

I started wondering why Africans had filled their minds and hearts with fear, ignorance, and superstition. I decided to find out if our belief in superstition and idolatry was worthwhile, and I eventually realized that belief in witches who were capable of siphoning off people's wealth and talents was not entirely true. The bulk of African superstitions can be violated with impunity. Many Africans go to good schools and universities to study science and perform scientific experiments, and then come out and practice superstition.

I faced much opposition when I tried to discuss the Bible with my friends. But I systematically improved my life with reason and common sense—those were the only weapons I had to discover the value of life. Keeping my rebellious thoughts to myself and wondering if there might be something wrong with me for doubting the existence of an Almighty God, I kept my eyes and mind open.

When I told my friends about my disappointment with Christianity, they tried to convince me to become a Muslim. But I knew that Islam would have been worse, because the degree of tolerance I enjoyed in Christianity was nonexistent in Islam.

Moreover, I knew that sooner or later I would be branded an infidel who would receive an infidel's punishment, and thus I did not accept Islam.

I didn't want to embrace an Eastern religion because, rather than make life easier for people, Eastern religionists engage in self-denial and unnecessary suffering. Therefore, having rejected such alternatives to Christianity, I felt alone with my mental predicament.

By this time I was twenty-four years old. One day in April 1991, I came home from Polytechnic for a weekend with my family. I saw a talk show on the television featuring two men. Norm R. Allen Jr., the executive director of African Americans for Humanism, was the guest speaker. What he said sounded very interesting and appealing to me, and immediately after the show, I told my sister that I had found where I belonged. She said I was crazy, but the next day I went to the office where the show originated and made inquiries as to how I could contact Allen. He left pamphlets and I got his address and was directed to Alex Attipoe of the Rational Centre in Accra, the Ghanaian capital.

Attipoe and I had a wonderful chat, and I decided to become a rationalist.

He lent me a couple of books which gave me a strong foundation in humanism. But the book that truly opened my eyes was *Man and His Gods* by Homer Smith. Later I received copies of *Free Inquiry* magazine from Allen, and I have enjoyed being a secular humanist ever since.

16.

PRAYING MY WAY TOWARD HUMANISM

David Allen

The question that I am constantly asked is how a born-again Christian could ever turn out to be a full-fledged humanist. The answer is simple. Too many letdowns, too many lies, too many contradictions, and too many hypocrites. Additionally, I learned to depend on myself to fulfill my needs and desires.

My faith in Christianity started to decline while I was still in middle school. I prayed for new clothes; I prayed for girlfriends; I prayed for money; I prayed for a bike. I prayed for many things. And though my prayers were never answered, I continued to have a strong belief in God. I was told—and believed—that God did not answer my prayers because I did not have enough faith.

Oddly enough, this belief was my first step toward humanism. I eventually received all of the material things for which I prayed. I obtained these things, however, through my own labor and abilities. I worked to earn money to buy a used bike from a friend. I found a job which paid me money with which to buy clothes. My belief in God was still strong, but I felt guilty because I was always asking him/her for ungodly things.

During my senior year in high school I was dealt a fatal blow to my faith. I was at football practice when I sustained a back injury. It was minor, but I was unable to go to practice. I could not go to summer football camp and was cut from the team. For years I had demonstrated a firm belief in God, and I figured he would come through for me in my time of need. I was watching Pat Robertson on the *700 Club* (as I did frequently), and he told the viewers who were ailing to pray with him and put their hands on their television sets. I did so. When the prayer was finished, my back felt better. I began to rejoice. I thanked the Lord. I danced and sang. I then collapsed with a more serious back injury. I asked myself, "Is there any truth to what I believe?"

The team I would have played for went undefeated that year. They were ranked number one in the metropolitan area. I wished that I could have shared the glory. Why would God not intervene for me? I no longer believed that I did not display enough faith. I was faithful, and no one could tell me differently. How much faith does it take? And how is faith being measured?

I began to think that God was not as powerful as I had assumed. I read the book *Chariots of the Gods* by Erich von Däniken. I began to think that God was nothing more than an extraterrestrial being who had just happened to come to Earth.

I also began formulating my own theories. I equated God with time. Those things that I believed God could deliver could also be delivered given enough time. Not even God could act without time. Time, in my opinion, was God. Once again, this was a big step toward humanism. By equating God with time I assumed that, in order to reach my goals, I would need time and effort.

The money that I always prayed for became available when I invested in the stock market and gave my investment time to grow. The car that I prayed for became available when I took time to save the money to purchase it. The girlfriend I prayed for was with me when I took the time to find her. I had found the answer!

Though I had drifted far to the left of Christianity, I still maintained some devotion to it. I felt that the Bible was still legitimate, but that it took time for things to occur. It took time for Moses to free the Jews. It took time for Jesus to prove his point. Therefore, I figured, Christianity should not be abandoned.

I maintained this philosophy until my brother, Norm Allen Jr., sent me a book titled *Atheism: The Case Against God,* by George H. Smith. I then realized that the Bible was filled with contradictions, absurdities, and blatant lies. I asked myself, "Why would Christians continue to tell these lies?" It then dawned on me that Christianity was a multitrillion dollar, international tax-free business. I realized that ministers were driving new Cadillacs and Mercedes Benzes while their benefactors could not even afford a one-bedroom efficiency apartment.

Greed is what perpetuates Christianity. Christian leaders are the biggest sinners of all! They are liars, cheats, extortionists, and sexual deviants. Their selling of religion to those who need a reprieve from the woes of daily living makes them no better than the cocaine dealer who is offering the same temporary relief. The only difference is that the Christian salesperson makes more money, sells it legally, and owes no taxes.

Today I am a firm believer in Darwin's theory of evolution. I am constantly being asked how I manage to live without believing in anything. I respond, "I believe in something. I believe in myself and humanity."

It has worked for me so far. But what if I am wrong? What if there is a God? What if there is a hell? And what if I go to hell? Well, because I will have an eternity, I will figure out a way to get myself into heaven.

17.

EMBRACING THE POWER OF HUMANISM

Gladman C. Humbles

I am a freethinker capable of capturing and controlling my own thoughts. My mind is open to change based on a theory that is logical, rational, reasonable, or proven.

I am not a crusader, cause champion, or crowd pleaser. While I have personally placed religion outside the realm of my life, I am not a Christian castigator. People should have the right to believe in whatever they choose, or to not believe at all. Why does one have to believe in a divine power rather than believe in the power of the person?

The decision to publish my experiences and thoughts was delayed out of fear—fear that the Christian community would ostracize, pressure, or proselytize. A Bible-believing Black Christian is the most acceptable and comforting African American to the American majority.

Thinking it out for yourself makes you "different." My decision to be different is based on my strong personality. I am not unselfish, obedient, unworthy, or meek, and I have one awesome ego! I am also compassionate and willing to extend my hand to help humanity within my capabilities.

I want to convince cliffhangers to seize the courage to come down to Earth and live a full, productive life in harmony with this planet. My complete concern is the direction of life and the survival of humankind on this planet.

The paranormal has always prodded me to ponder and probe phenomena that seemed incomprehensible. Curiosity, inquisitiveness, and rebelliousness have always been prominent in my personality. Santa's ability to traverse the universe and crawl through the chimneys of the world in one night was a bit much for my young mind to handle. My parents were probed and pressured into sacking Santa and satisfying me with sane, sensible answers.

My move from the religious realm was motivated by experiencing personal tragedy and thought-provoking mental battles within my mind. There were three major problems:

1. Coerced church attendance as a child and young adult while living with a relative. There was no choice. Forcing me to conform always stirred my rebellious spirit.
2. A mother who died at forty who was hooked on prayer and "faith healing" rather than proven medical methods.
3. A son who fell under the spell of a charlatan charmer. The charmer lived a kingly earthly life while his flock floundered in poverty, awaiting their "kingdom" in heaven.

My mental battles were won after a study of history, personal experiences, and observations. Following were some of my thoughts:

1. Slavery was scripturally justified. Why slaves adopted the religion of savage slavemasters who treated animals better than their slaves is beyond my comprehension.
2. Caucasian Christians collectively have never accepted African Americans as equals—and never will.

3. How much wealth would African Americans own if church contributions had been placed in General Motors, Ford, and Chrysler stock?

4. A caring Christian father would never let one of his children go hungry at a table of plenty. Our all-good, all-caring, and all-powerful heavenly father allows millions of the world's children to go hungry every night. Thousands of African children die daily after slow, steadfast, sorrowful suffering. Their only sin was being born. What is the rationale? Are poverty-stricken children his children, or did God go to sleep?

5. Job suffered severely as a test of faith according to the Bible. Job is often quoted as a measure of how strong and lasting one's faith is. An all-knowing God allows those he knows are going to be faithful and remain loyal to the end to suffer the same fate as agnostics and atheists. It would seem logical to take the faithful to heaven before the suffering starts. "God knows best" is the answer I have always been given when there is no logical explanation.

6. Why would God entrust his message to Matthew, Mark, Luke, and John? These were obscure men who wrote the gospels of Jesus Christ many years after his death. They have no recorded history or biography. The people are asked to take it on the trust of four men who say they were divinely inspired. If you take my message meaningfully, you should demand proof of my statements of fact, question my convictions with logic, and make up your own mind which direction you desire to travel.

7. My mind belongs to me. Whatever decisions I make, good or bad, my decisions are my own. I am not about to give credit to some unseen spirit for motivating my mind. I will take credit for the good decisions and full responsibility for the bad ones. Sooner or later churchgoing Christians are going to leave their minds at home. If God told the preacher what to tell you, you must accept it completely, reject it, reject part of it, and/or read your Bible for yourself. If you comprehend differently, you must stay in your church in a frustrated state, find a new church, or start one.

8. The childlike mentality of being told when to sit, stand, sing, and raise hands to answer simple questions is reminiscent of kindergarten. What logic is there in a ritual that reduces an adult's mentality to childlike thinking, except to limit and restrict one's ability to think for oneself and to make one obey without question?

9. Why are Christians commanded to go out and compel people to come to Christ? After nearly two thousand years of mass indoctrination it seems rational that the people would be banging on doors of overcrowded churches asking God to let them in.

10. The Bible has been used by some to promote brotherhood and by others to promote bigotry. How can two such diametrically opposed ideas be interpreted to such extremes from a book that is supposed to tell us clearly how to live?

In conclusion, challenging changes and conditions on Earth is at times frustrating, exciting, painful, pleasurable, ravaging, rapturous. I would not have it any other way. I do not want to be happy all the time, nor do I desire to be loved by everyone. For me, living as some blissful spirit for eternity would be a duller existence than being in the other place.

And why should one be concerned with how it all began? I do not know how it all began and I don't care. I am here, you are here. Why can't we learn to think differently, look differently, live differently, and live in harmony with humankind and nature, making the best of it on this planet?

18.

FROM CHRISTIANITY TO SANITY

Anthony Burnside

I was born into a partially religious and superstitious family. But I was always a precocious child. I had an intense curiosity about everything.

My mother took my brother and me to church every Sunday and Wednesday evening. I was about ten years old when I had my first Holy Ghost experience. I was sitting in a pew with my brother when a woman jumped up and howled as if she had sat on a pin. She stared into space and chanted, "Oh, Jesus!" My brother and I stared at this woman as if she had descended from heaven—it was very emotional.

That was the red-letter day in my life when I accepted Jesus as my personal savior—and that was when the trouble began.

I started attending church and began my training as a soldier of Jesus, as they would call it. We had intense Bible studies. I even joined the local Youth For Christ (YFC) Club. I went to school telling children "Jesus loves you." I walked and talked the Bible, and of course this behavior caused me to be a social outcast. But I did not care, because Jesus was my friend—or so I thought.

By this time I had discovered girls and developed an interest in magic and magicians. In the years that followed I acquired knowledge about certain aspects of my religion from a secular viewpoint. This was a shock to my belief system. Three years had passed since my acceptance of Jesus, and my life had not changed at all. I was still an outcast. I felt alienated from my family, and I started to delve into illusions and the New Age. The church told me that I was a child of Satan for practicing magic, but I never stopped.

But then came a turning point in my life. I became confused about what I believed; but I still adhered to the teachings of Christianity out of fear. I was in Sunday school learning the story of David and Bathsheba. After the story was told, the teachers went to the back room. I heard so much lewd conversation about the story that I thought, "This is not happening to me." At that moment I felt something leave me. I was never the same again.

I started living the life of a religious hypocrite. This new persona came about partly because Jesus was not fulfilling my prayers. I started questioning everything with the same fervor I had as a Christian. I was ridiculed, insulted, and called Satan's child simply for questioning the Scriptures.

I continued to read the Bible. But I was told that I did not read it correctly. I told the ministers about the contradictions surrounding the creation story. They scoffed at me. This upset me because I did not think that a preacher would be crippled by impenetrable ignorance.

I eventually discovered Islam, but not the orthodox form. I joined the infamous Nation of Islam (NOI). I left the NOI after a while because I could no longer accept the "White man is the devil" ideology.

One day, a fellow Muslim and I were standing on a street corner. A White man fell from his motorcycle. I rushed to a pay phone to call for help, but my Muslim friend said, "Show a White man no mercy, because they didn't show mercy to your slave mother and father." Though I was confused, I agreed. We repeatedly chanted, "Die! White devil, die! White devil!"

I was taught that all White people are evil—they were all grafted from an evil being. Therefore, I disrespected my White school-teachers. This hatred was destroying me inside, so I left the NOI. I felt much better, though I did not know where my life was headed.

I was introduced to orthodox Islam by a Palestinian woman I dated briefly. I was impressed; no one forced anything down my throat, as in Christianity. But I had a problem with the theology, though I warmly embraced the humanist message of Al-Islam.

In January of 1991 I met a man who changed my life forever—Verle Muhrer, my philosophy instructor. I hated him when we first met, and I dropped his class. But later I reluctantly gave him a chance—and I am glad I did.

As I got to know him I learned that my secularism was okay, that I was not crazy. I no longer felt ashamed of my secular side. Indeed, I felt proud. Finally, I had meaning in my life. I felt as if a load of bricks had been lifted off my back.

I was invited to a humanist meeting at Verle's home. I was flab-bergasted to see a picture of Malcolm X on his wall. (I do not know many Whites who have pictures of Malcolm X on their walls.) That night I learned a new word, "Eupraxophy," which means living the good life guided by reason and philosophy. Verle gave me books about Robert Ingersoll, Bertrand Russell, Paul Kurtz, and others. I absorbed everything I read. The book that had the greatest impact on me was *The Transcendental Temptation*, by Paul Kurtz. I have always contended that if books were cars, this book would be a Cadillac or a Rolls Royce.

Verle Muhrer helped a great deal and saved me from a lot of mental turmoil. And today I am proud to be a freethinker.

19.

MAKING AN EASY AND NATURAL TRANSITION

Chaka Ferguson

There was no revelation, no conversion, no traumatic life experience that turned me to secular humanism. It was more of a gradual progression in my life, from irreligion to the outright rejection of the religious and the supernatural.

To this day, I could never really say what exactly turned me off to religion. Maybe I was never turned on to it in the first place.

I was raised in a sort of irreligious household, where religion was neither promoted nor discouraged. Seldom did my family discuss religion. My parents allowed me to attend church and to look to other religions or to no religion at all.

Since we never talked about religion, I do not really know what my parents or my siblings believe when it comes to the supernatural. It just was not a topic of discussion in our home.

But, like any other city, my hometown of Miami was full of religionists. And I would have my fair share of run-ins with them.

While I cannot say what turned me off religion, I definitely know what has kept me away from it—religionists.

If religion is trying to sell itself, its representatives don't market it very well.

(For example, I once told a Christian that I was happily married, and that no nonexistent god had anything to do with the love between my wife and myself. She remarked that the devil gives gifts too, insinuating that my wife was somehow betrothed to me by Satan himself! I think this absurd statement speaks for itself.)

At the behest of a few friends interested in "saving my soul," however, I attended church on several occasions to see what I was missing out on, which, to say the least, was not much.

I could see by the circus-type atmosphere in the church (the usual Holy Ghost possessions, etc.) that I was not buying the bill of goods the preacher was selling. Being raised pretty much as a freethinker, I was not brainwashed into accepting what the church elders had to say, and would question my friends about the ridiculous and illogical statements that were made during the service.

Why would you thank Jesus for being fired from work or being kicked out of your home, or with coming down with a cold? Can you define God? And why would you praise a deity who admitted in his own Bible that he created evil? Why would you worship a deity that ordered all types of atrocities? Who is, by his own admission, vengeful and jealous? Who is perfect, yet had to create beings to make him happy, albeit imperfect beings? Who commits mass murder and genocide (the Genesis flood)?

Obviously their answers were the usual, tired Christian ones: You have to have faith; you have to open your heart to God; you cannot try to use logic to explain God; How can you have love without God?

Put your money in the plate, pass it on, no questions asked. Sounds like the perfect con game.

I soon found that "why" is the most troublesome word in the world for religionists.

Following my brief tryout with Christianity—well, it was not much of a tryout in the first place, since I never considered myself a Christian—I flirted with Islam for a short time.

My first introduction to Islam was through the Nation of Islam, while I was in college. Like many Black collegians, I was immediately attracted to Afrocentric studies and philosophies. I became immersed in Black history and earned a minor in African American studies.

While Black studies provides an intellectual framework for African American sociopolitical thought, African American programs on most college campuses are a haven for all types of dogmatic Black groups, such as the Nation of Islam and its rival splinter groups (the 5 Percent Nation, for example).

Here I got my first dose of militant Black theology, which, if the colors were reversed, would be White supremacist theology. While my professors stuck to political, historical, and social issues, many of these groups would boast about how they were "the gods and goddesses" of the world and the "original people," whatever that means.

Yet these "gods and goddesses" could do no more than spew vitriol about how the "White man" was some "grafted devil." If I could not accept the absurdities of the Christian creation myth and its assorted miracles, I would have been a hypocrite to accept this equally absurd Black Muslim theology of how a mad scientist created the White race.

Orthodox Muslims told me that the Nation of Islam and its rival splinter groups did not practice "true" Islam. So, now more skeptical than ever, I gave the orthodox Muslims a shot, to be fair.

But the contradictions that popped up in Christianity also popped up in Islam. Free will vs. omnipotence. An all-good God vs. a world full of evil. A holy book full of contradictions. And then there are the followers, with their petty schisms and differing interpretations of the Word.

This is despite the fact that orthodox Islam, even more so than Christianity and the Nation of Islam, is ultrasexist and homophobic.

And when I asked the Muslims—be they Nation of Islam or orthodox—the same questions about God, they usually responded with the same convoluted logic, contradictions, and rationalizations as the Christians.

I would choose either self-delusion or sanity. My progression toward humanism was moving forward rapidly.

After a brief period of reflection and study, I discovered that all along I was a humanist. I had always questioned religion, always questioned the existence of gods, always been skeptical of the metaphysical and supernatural.

I never looked to the supernatural for solutions to my problems. I never blamed malevolent spirits for my failures. I never needed a superman in the sky to tell me that I should treat other people fairly and with respect. I did not need a fairy-tale book full of contradictions and absurdities to teach me how to live.

In fact, I believe the humanist actually has a deeper appreciation of life. With no promise of a future afterlife of eternal bliss or torture, the humanists are forced to make do with what they have now on Earth. Since we do not know if things are going to get better after we die, we try to make the world better in the present.

Humanists do not have a false sense of duty. They try to improve the condition of humanity not because they feel obligated, but because they know this is all we have, and as far as we can determine, this is the only chance we have to do things right.

Humanism has no doctrines or dogmatic creeds. Its adherents do not blindly accept any ideology. The humanist is open-minded, always seeking answers, and does not accept faith as proof or evidence for the existence of anything. In short, humanism embraces freethought.

I have always placed my faith, if it can be called that, in the scientific method and rational inquiry. I know that humans may never answer every question about life. There may be no answers to some of them.

But that does not mean that because we do not know—or cannot know—we should stop pursuing knowledge, or make up nonexistent deities to explain away our ignorance of the universe.

My path to humanism was not fraught with the ups and downs that usually accompany those who travel to humanism from some sort of religion. I had always been a humanist. I had always embraced its ideals. I had always promoted its spirit. I just did not know what to call what I was living.

Now I do.

20.

REFLECTIONS ON RELIGION AND HUMANISM

Charles W. Faulkner

I grew up in a family that was close to the church. Regular Sunday school and church attendance was a family tradition. It is funny, though, that I cannot recall my mother being so fervently attached to the church as was my grandmother. This lack of mindless devotion to the church was revealed in the way that my mother raised me.

For instance, my mother married my stepfather while I was a child. My stepfather was old-fashioned and, in the old-fashioned tradition, he wanted me to help him tend to his garden. My mother said (I can recall her exact words), "Charles doesn't want to be working in anybody's garden."

This statement exemplified her commonsense way of looking at life. I spent many hours playing basketball—sometimes twelve hours per day "tossing buckets." My mother never interfered with my athletic endeavors. She even supported my fifteen-year amateur boxing career. She cheered me on. She seemed to be more in touch with reality than were most of her peers. She and I never discussed this, and I do not know why she felt the way that she did.

During my early and teen years, fights, robberies, muggings, gang violence, and racism made my early faith in religion diminish quickly. I doubted that God could protect us and make this a better world. Violence was the only common denominator.

Physical dominance was all that most people understood. Yet people prayed while conditions steadily deteriorated. On the basketball court, in the boxing ring, in many homes, and on the street, the stronger person dominated. (Not the most religious, but the most powerful.)

The poor Black folks in the South prayed while their homes were being burned down by the Ku Klux Klan. Whites attended church devotedly, but would not allow Blacks to worship with them. The same upstanding citizens often used the Bible to justify racism.

When I presented these issues to officials of my church, they told me to pray. When I became persistent and displayed dissatisfaction with this tactic, they told me that I should enroll in a Bible study class that would give me the knowledge that I need about our world under God. I enrolled in the Unitarian Church, however, because of my belief that its doctrine viewed Jesus as a historical figure—human like the rest of us. My activities with the Unitarian Church were short-lived, however, because I did not cater to the ceremony of the speech-sermon. I was therefore left without a philosophical home.

At this time I was a struggling college student in search of a major. I tried English, history, and practically every other area of study. When I took the required courses in logic and introduction to philosophy, I found an area of extraordinary interest.

I understood much more clearly the diversity of ideas and some of the reasons underlying them. I knew where I stood in the evolution of social thought. I no longer felt like a philosophical outcast. I was in good company, but how could I label myself? I could have labeled myself existentialist, atheist, pragmatist, realist, humanist, or all of the above. I put my social thought into action with trips on the "Freedom Bus" to the Deep South, in order to encourage frightened citizens of Mississippi, South Carolina, and Arkansas to vote.

Since that time I have been strongly opposed to having an idea forced upon me which I either disagree with or cannot justify with logic. I have fought diligently for the right of people to believe as they wish, as long as their ideas do not limit the freedom of others. During my studies in philosophy and social thought, I discovered the many ways that one could be made to accept a specific idea. The intellectual, conscious method is the most prominent. With respect to religion, many people fear the consequences (such as "hell") if they do not accept the belief in God.

Another major method of influencing one's behavior, without having him consciously accept an idea, is through brainwashing or behavioral manipulation. If one sees a slice of cake on television, or a box of popcorn at the movies, one might develop a desire for the particular food. People usually think that the desire originated on its own, rather than through an idea that someone else initiated.

This powerful means of behavioral control is common. I wanted to learn everything about it that I could. This manipulative methodology is the underlying element in religion. It makes one believe in the power of prayer for relaxation. In reality, however, the individual is using his mind to control and relax himself. Thus, God is actually in one's mind. Nevertheless, when one accepts conventional religion, he is giving over control of himself to someone else (usually a pastor).

This discovery threw me entirely into the camp of humanism. Humanism allows individuals to be their own persons and to use their own minds to achieve an important place in the universe. I always ask questions, and I become immediately skeptical when others refrain from answering them or defer to faith and mythology. For many adults, Santa Claus still exists, in the form of astrology, palmistry, superstition, and mysticism.

There are those who profess to be humanists, however, who espouse racial and ethnic prejudices. "I am a humanist, but I really do wish more Black people were motivated like the rest of us." "I want to hire more Black young people to work for me, but I can't find any good ones." "Hispanic people are very loving. It's too bad that so many of them use drugs."

These remarks are so prejudicial as to be dehumanizing. Yet the proponents of the philosophies that support these statements tend to believe that they are nice people who believe in serving humanity. The problem is that they do not think that minorities are fully human. Thus, in their view, their ideas are acceptable in humanistic terms. This inane justification of prejudice and accompanying discrimination makes useful and important the cliché, "Never judge a book by its cover." Never judge a humanist by his smile.

During the early days of slavery in the United States, some of the finest citizens of outstanding moral character condoned slavery. They are now considered the fathers of democracy—the founders of freedom. Yet many of them were slaveholders. They fought for equality but they kept slaves. That is contradictory, isn't it?

From their point of view, it was not at all contradictory. White people were first-class citizens. Slaves were regarded as little more than cattle. The Constitution was not written to give them freedom or to protect it. Thus, the founders saw no contradiction. They had taken it upon themselves to classify the human species.

Some humanists have taken a similar tack. By placing themselves in a select, superior category, they can criticize other humans and still consider themselves humanists. For example, an upstanding humanist and president of a large company felt comfortable saying publicly at a humanist convention: "I want to hire Black youngsters, but all of those I hire are lazy. They just don't want to work."

To correctly label oneself a humanist certainly requires a philosophy and moral requirement far greater than the one indicated above.

21.

CROSSING THE BORDER IN A GOLDEN SEARCH
A Testimony on Personal Enlightenment

Alfred T. Kisubi

Thinking about my personal enlightenment compels memories of the unfolding pattern of my life, with its crossroads and initiation rituals of birth, school, and college in Uganda, and graduate school in the American Midwest, which for me have been milestones to signal where I've been or should be, and point to a new direction and distance ahead to new destinations in a golden search. My childhood in Uganda, my young adulthood teaching in Kenya, and my middle adulthood adjunct instructorship in philosophy and, subsequently, human services associate professorship in the United States, have been the essence of this unfolding pattern. The type of education I got and the credentials earned along the way are the milestones which at each stage opened up new directions for me.

What a golden search!

THE GOLDEN SEARCH*

Today, facing the ceaseless rhythm of time
I pause to think,
What golden search life is!
For seven years my virgin childhood,
Like the lamb the shepherd
Followed daily orders, "Do this, not that!"
For four years new ideas hatched in me
An inhibited self rocked inside me,
In a tremendous metamorphosis.

Two more years, a dilemma grasped me
Testing my humanhood,
To go or not to go on . . .
Always's the challenge.

Work, not fortune earned me three years
Of golden search for humanhood and identity
Sixteen serious years,
I searched, then sighed,
But only briefly;
For again, here I am, searching,
Again and again, along
A mystical solitary journey
Always ahead of us.

(Alfred Kisubi, 1983)

In this search I have greatly benefited from the methods of inquiry that each discipline taught me. The social and physical sciences taught me to search and research like a prospector probing the crust in a golden search, the arts equipped me with the tools to define priorities and pursue those that matter. Studying about the Afrocentric humanist movement, which intensified after World War II as the guiding prin-

---

*Reprinted by permission of *Portfolio*, Johnson County Community College, 1986.

ciple to African freedom fighters, intellectuals and a few Western liberals enhanced my African personality. Knowing about negritude, African socialism or *ujamaa*, pan-Africanism, nationalism, and currently Molefi Asante's Afrocentricity (all forms of the Afrocentric humanist movement) with the spirit of early modern philosophy, with its empiricisms and rationalisms, produced in me an attitude of independent intellectual inquiry, like it did for many African intellectuals.

The concept of human dignity occurs to me again and again as Africans continue to seek to establish an African world presence and to gain the respect for our own way of life. To many Africanists this comes in many forms—the study and performance of traditional music, dance, and sculpture, the writing of African history, the search for a fresh African idiom in contemporary artistic expression, the reshaping of Western-style educational standards and values, the turning to indigenous forms of Christianity (or opting for Afrocentric secularism), and the continuing debate over national languages.

To me human dignity came through my education at Isegero Catholic Primary School, Busowa Catholic Junior Secondary School, Kiira (Anglican) College, Jinja, St. Peter's (Catholic) College, Tororo, and Makerere University, Kampala, Uganda, and the University of Missouri-Kansas City. Through my vocational training in teaching, which earned me an Uganda Ministry of Education Certificate in teaching comparative religion (Christianity and African religions, geography, and English/literature), I was able to scrutinize the nature of religion vis-à-vis the sciences and arts. Studying animal husbandry at Entebbe Veterinary Institute in Uganda equipped me with more research and theoretical/practical skills in agricultural/tannery biochemistry, agronomy, and animal production. By the time I went to Makerere University to study political science, philosophy, sociology, and literature, that university, like other modern African universities, had for over a decade undergone a sea drift away from the curricula bequeathed by colonial administrators toward one suited to African needs. Institutes of African studies examined the old arts and experimented with the new, scholars explored past civilizations and present politics, while departments of pedagogy debated the degree and nature of schooling needed to put sinew into developing societies.

Here I am again, vying for a new credential as a confirmed skeptic and humanist. At this point, as I reveal myself in my true humanist colors, as a stick-in-the-mud, I hold a number of beliefs that have been embraced by the liveliest intellects of our species: Auguste Comte, Thoreau, Walter Whitman, Gandhi, Martin Luther King Jr., Kenneth Clark, Paul Fraire, and Julius Nyerere, to name a few. With them I believe that order is better than chaos, creation better than destruction. I prefer gentleness to violence, forgiveness to vendetta. On the whole, like Socrates and Plato, I think that knowledge is better than ignorance, and I am sure that human sympathy is more valuable than ideology. I believe that in spite of the recent triumphs of science, humans haven't changed much in the last two thousand years; and in consequence, we must still try to learn from history. History is ourselves. I also hold one or two beliefs that are more difficult to state briefly. For example, I believe in courtesy, the ritual by which we avoid hurting other people while satisfying our own egos. And I think we should remember that we are part of a great whole, which for convenience we call the world. All people and other living things are our brothers and sisters. Above all, like Jean-Jacques Rousseau, John Locke, Thomas Hobbes, Thomas Jefferson, and Abraham Maslow, I believe in the endowed genius of all individuals, regardless of gender, race, age, socioeconomic status, or handicap; and I value a society or a discipline, such as humanism, that makes their existence possible. These beliefs are the infrastructure upon which my philosophy of humanism is based. I also believe in the quantitative scientific method for gathering and analyzing empirical data, but I think that we should triangulate this with alternative methodologies, such as qualitative and participative observation, and other epistemologies, such as case studies, tenacity, ethnomethodology, and ethnography.

After my finals at Makerere University Kampala, I boarded a bus back to Jinja, my hometown, equipped with Afrocentric humanism. The many roadblocks manned by cantankerous soldiers between the capital and my home district made a strong statement to me that all was not well in my country. My native land was far from peace and set out for incessant war, even after the fall of dictator Idi Amin. The reign of terror was so entrenched in the blood of our leaders it would take the martyrdom of more and more of us to surmount the mayhem. I determined not to be one of those martyrs, though. As the hot bus snaked and bounced its way on the Eastern Uganda Highway, my mind scanned the possibilities that lay ahead. After all, the sun rose in the East. As a wise man from the East, I had achieved the coveted upper-second in sociology and political science with a minor in literature. Possibly I stood a chance of getting on the wrecked train that was the Uganda civil service. And maybe not, because three hundred arts/social science majors had graduated that year and done their Civil Service interviews, in which they vied for a miserable ten positions that timidly peeped at us in the half-page classified section of the new postwar newspaper clips pinned on the university notice boards.

But I had nothing to worry about, if the civil service was looking for meritorious candidates. I had an upper-second bachelor's degree! Surely the government would choose me for merit above those who had barely made lower-second, or worse still a mere pass degree, which was looked down upon by mainstream Makererians as "the (lazy) gentle-man/ gentle-lady degree." At the interview one of the people from the Civil Service Commission was a man from my district, who not only spoke Lusoga, my native tongue, but belonged to my paternal kinship and lineage of the Baise Igaga clan of the buffalo totem. The Basoga, just like the Abagusii of Kenya, belong to the Bantu group, which includes many ethnic groups inhabiting a vast portion of the African continent, mostly in eastern, central, and southern Africa. The Basoga's habitat for millennia has been the northern shores of *Enhandha* (or *Nyanza*) (Lake) *Nalubaale*, which the Europeans renamed after their divine-powered Queen Victoria. I grew up twenty miles north of this massive lake.

The man at the interview several weeks later saw me at the Crested Towers trying to check on the results of the interview. He said, "*Muna twakwima omulimo* (Buddy, we begrudged you the position). *Abacholi bagutwaala!*" (The Acholis took it!). Behind his grin I saw the invisible predicament of Uganda's nationhood. Brotherhood was thicker than nationhood. The Acholi are a northern Ugandan ethnic group that dominated the army, the civil service, and politics in those days.

So as the bus squeaked to a stop at the Jinja bus depot, over the clanging and banging of the tinkers' hammers in the nearby market I heard a remote voice of a nation beaten out of shape. No doubt the hyena of injustice was on the loose to get me. I had to run fast. Dart into a safe place or be masticated. Surely there must be some safe haven in my own hometown. I had called Jinja College, where my cousin-in-law was the headmaster. He immediately offered me a temporary position to teach literature and Christian religious education to candidates of the national Ordinary Level exams. Before I took his offer I called J. R., the headmaster of Kiira College, Butiki, my alma mater. J. R. lived in my dormitory when he and I attended the school he now administered. He was a Musoga like me, and although his higher education had been done in Canada, he remembered me from high-school days, and chances were that as Basoga, we both faced the hyena of injustice from the dominant ethnic groups. Maybe we could sink or swim together, as Old Boys and Basoga.

Subsequently Kiira College, Butiki became the best bet. They had a farm, so milk that was scarce elsewhere in the country would be available to all instructors and school employees at a token price. Once in a while one of the swine or even the beef cattle would be culled and slaughtered for the waiting palates of the students and school employees. Occasionally there were relief sardines that the European Economic Community (EEC) funneled to the school through the corrupt government mechanism. In civil war Uganda, Kiira college was heaven, so I decided to return to the hill where I was academically raised, to teach the next generation.

I took the chance one evening. J. R. picked me up in the school truck driven by the old man Mpata, who was first hired as a school driver when I was a student at the school in the late 1960s. So when he showed up at my Jinja Main Street residence, which I rented from Busoga Diocese, Mpata was surprised to see how big I had become. He and I reminisced about old times, and did more of this with J. R. when the three of us sped uphill on the murram road to Kiira College, leaving behind us a cloud of dust.

On arrival I was very glad I had returned to my alma mater. It was different this time though. I was not paying fees and lining up to get supplies. Instead I was moving into the house that during my student years belonged to the headmaster, Mr. Freak, the English man who had been one of the founders of the school. He and his wife acted like typical Anglican missionaries. She was the school nurse. He was a lay reader, who loved both preaching the gospel and teaching us boys: physics, sex education, marriage and family based on middle class English norms, judo, gymnastics, and, of course, Scottish dance. The Freaks also advised the school branch of the national Uganda Students Scripture Union Fellowship (USSUF). I joined the fellowship, and in my senior year became a Christian leader, in which capacity I chaperoned junior boys (brothers) to born-again fellowships at other schools. I wrote Christian letters, Bible lessons, and sermons. My cousin, who also belonged to USSUF, became an Anglican priest. But I was more interested in writing secular stories and poems—in English, of course. Those were the days when speaking our language was punishable by being gated or performing manual labor, and our ethnic beliefs and customs were disdained, and as a result rejected by some of us who were Western-educated. Those were indeed the days when education was a process of systematic effort through which our teachers, European or African, actively worked on assimilating us into Western culture, without regard for the villages to which we would eventually return. It was not long before all educated Africans realized that although school exposed us to new ideas and ways, we couldn't forget our African culture and tradition as still practiced in the life of our parents and grandparents. We had to come to terms with the cultural conflict that loomed ahead of each of us between African values and Western values, between the old and the new. For example, modern medical doctors and their medicine versus local medicine practitioners (herbalists) and their potions.

My teaching at Kiira College lasted two months. One night Lubowa, a young enterprising physicist I had met earlier at St. James Secondary School, came to the house J. R. had allocated to me—Mr. Freak's house. When I opened the door for him, Lubowa greeted me with his usual irony. "Are you the Black Mr. Freak?" he asked. "Yes," I returned the joke, "if you mean taking over this house. No way!" I said with a knot in my throat, "If you mean the teaching. I don't think Scottish dance is relevant to us anymore, if it ever was while the Freaks lived in this house. All we need is peace in Uganda. We must have peace and tranquility to practice our own cultures. Give us calm and take away this storm that sounds like the Bujagali Falls on the Nile that I hear every night." Through the window Lubowa looked out at the Nile River glittering five miles away. He said, "We need consensus which flows like the river."

The next morning I took Lubowa outside to see what used to be the Freaks' lawn. All the flower gardens were gone. Someone who lived here after the Freaks had planted an orchard instead. Annuals and biennials were growing side by side, happily preparing their fruits and roots for human consumption. The change in this lawn signified the differences between European and African tastes. The conflict of cultures could not have had any more graphic depiction than this.

But Uganda had another conflict to contain or be consumed by: the ethnic rivalry that had plunged us into a civil war. We Ugandans—Baganda, Kakwa, Nubi, Langi, Acholi, Basoga, Bagishu, Karamojong, Banyoro, Batoro, Banyankore—we Ugandans were busy at each others' throats in an endless carnage masked as a war of liberation. The martyrdom I was scared of was creeping closer and closer to all of us. I was not going to sit waiting for it to come to Kiira College.

Lubowa told me that I could come with him to Kenya and escape for a while from the purging and vendetta that stalked every Ugandan. He pushed me while I was squatting—it was not hard for him to knock me down prostrate. Soon I agreed to escape to Kenya. Under the circumstances, nothing was better. "Take the opportunity or die!" I thought. To get across the Uganda-Kenya border at Busia (seventy miles east of Jinja), Lubowa and I crammed ourselves into a *matatu* (taxi) carrying smugglers and peddlers who were also headed for the promise in the East. In about an hour the matatu arrived at the border. Lubowa and I alighted. He had a cramp in his left leg and I had a stitch in my stomach caused by the tension in the taxi. Soon Lubowa led the way to the border. Given my size (even at forty my American students say I look twenty) I appeared too small and insignificant to be checked at the border. So, clutching my concealed Bachelor of Arts diploma, I crossed into Kenya. A woman whom Lubowa introduced to me helped bring across my scanty luggage. It was wise to travel lightly during those days of roadblocks and highway robberies.

"Can you teach Christian religious education (CRE), or literature?" Lubowa asked me as our bus sped on its way deep into the warm heart of Kenya. "Positive! But I would prefer something more tangible and empirical, like literature or social science or a combination," I said. Later I learned that Lubowa had started a personal campaign to recruit teachers from war-torn Uganda and take them to safety in Kenya. I was his latest catch, and I loved his fishing!

At Nyamagwa Catholic Mission, Lubowa introduced me to the headmaster, Father Onkanga, in a manner that showed me that he had brought to Kenya a good number of Ugandan teachers. Whatever his reasons were, I had no time to ask him. I was too preoccupied with getting away from the Ugandan storm to bother asking him. "Can you teach Christian religious education (CRE) or literature?" Father Onkanga asked. "Both, Father, but I would rather teach literature!" I replied. "You see, Father . . . I'm curious about the Abagusii!" I added. In many aspects they're like my own ethnic group— the Basoga of eastern Uganda. They say, "*Abwo!*" (Here!); we say, "*Awo!*" They call water "*amache*"; we call it "*amadhi.*" Their language sounds like corrupted Lusoga (or is Lusoga corrupted Ekegusii?). However, there were many differences in practices and even language. Soon I realized that my adventures in Kisii and the rest of Kenya must be recorded and studied, so that I could come to terms with the subtle and not-so-subtle similarities and differences between my host culture and my native culture. The more Lubowa took me to meet more and more Abagusii individuals and families, and the more I attended their ceremonies, the more I was enticed to study the *ekegusii* oral literature so that I could appreciate it, in order to appreciate its composers better—not only as my neighbors in the East African community, but also as fellow human beings. Besides, Father Onkanga hired me to teach literature because the Kenya National Examinations Council (KNEC) included African oral literature in the syllabi for Ordinary and Advanced Levels, which I thought was a mature and timely rejection of the early chauvinistic Eurocentric attitude. It was a recognition of the fact that anything true to art in

African oral literature is good, and needs to be improved upon for the transformation of African society in a Nyererian "Education for Self-reliance."[1] There I was, my Afrocentric humanist mission before me. Researching Abagusii oral literature would be the way to inject its aspects into what I taught, in order to ameliorate the pitiable conflict in thought and attitude between the young and the old which derived from the early missionary education, which alienated the young school-goer from indigenous heritage by degrading it and denouncing it as false, evil, pagan, or unholy.

My students and I set out to identify the different genres, such as stories (*Emegano*), proverbs (*Emebeyano*), riddles (*Ebitendawiri*), and poems, both epic and lyric (*Esimbore, emeino, ebirero, amagombo*). We tried to understand the issues raised in the different genres and to isolate any relationship between those issued in every genre and those raised in a different genre.

We made an effort to understand the content of any genre and the context in which the compositions were relayed. We discussed plot, narratives, themes and ideas, language, and characters and their contextual relationship with one another. Above all we appreciated the forms used: the narrative techniques, language, diction, creation of atmosphere, mood, tone, and all the literary devices used in every composition. Because oral tradition formed a great part of the Abagusii culture with elders transmitting by word of mouth to the young ones the customs, beliefs, and expectations of their heritage, we carried out research on the relevance of oral literature to Kisii life. We tried to match the genres we discovered with the pertinent concerns of society. We infiltrated the social environment in which the oral literature is presented. My students were encouraged to physically hunt for occasions such as birth, initiation, marriage, burial, and so on. We discussed why oral literature was dramatized on such occasions. We also tried to compare Kisii performances with those of other parts of Africa, especially East Africa. Expressed in most of this literature was the evidence that there are cultural links between the peoples of Africa. Lastly, we were interested in finding out what use this literature was to society.

We tried to find out what the children gained through listening to legends, myths, folktales, folk songs, and proverbs, and in participating in or observing the dances. For five years my students set out every holiday, equipped with a questionnaire to help them gather information. We were an army of humanists, applying the scientific method to Kisii data in a bid to popularize and disseminate knowledge, expressed in common terms for common service, and in the language of the people. The humanists Africa needs are for here and now. Humanists will provide sustainable services to the poor and hungry, empower the people to meet the needs that confront them, respond to the crises of drought and flood, and also to the multiple appeals from individuals and communities who normally lack basics that the rest of the world, including the African elite, take for granted (sufficient food, adequate shelter, and the opportunity for people to achieve these by themselves). The mosques and churches have carried out similar missions on the continent for years, but as Mzee Kenyatta once said, "When the missionaries came, we had the land and they had the Bible in hand; they then told us to kneel down and pray, closing our eyes; when we opened our eyes a century later, they had our land and we had their Bibles in hand."

Please note that my varied and extensive study of Western and non-Western (African) political science/philosophy, sociology, and literature, at undergraduate level, and Western sociology (emphasis on sociological theory, research methods, gerontology, complex organizations, crime and deviance, human development, marriage and family, the interdisciplinary approach to problems of developmental disability [DD] and mental retardation [MR]), and my majoring in American administration of higher education at graduate level comprise the interdisciplinary database from which I retrieve the concepts, methodologies, and the philosophy for my research designs and teaching techniques. I have a moral obligation to be skeptical and to demand evidence for all statements that claim to be facts. Surely we Africans should require no less of ourselves and of those who come to plunder our continent. Show Me before I Believe is my motto.

NOTE

1. *Editor's note:* Julius Nyerere led Tanganyika to independence in 1961. He was president in Tanganyika (1961–64) and then president of Tanzania (1964–85).

22.

THE BLACK HUMANIST EXPERIENCE
An Alternative to Religion

Norm R. Allen Jr.

When I was a young child, my parents and grandparents sent me to church on Sundays. And like any other sensible, red-blooded American boy, I hated it. But what could I do? Freedom of religion and freedom *from* religion are not guaranteed to children.

The insufferable drivel of the preaching parasites in their pulpits bored me almost to tears. I would pray that God would shut them up. But, alas, these prayers were never answered, and I simply had to grit my teeth and bear my unjust punishment (talk about child abuse!).

The worst thing that ever happened to me as a Baptist was the psychological torment I experienced as a result of embracing the belief in hell. I worried constantly about being consumed by flames because I had sinned and angered the perfectly loving God. To compound this utterly groundless and irrational fear, I was learning about competing religions that also proclaimed that those who did not accept *their* one true God would face eternal torment. For a young child, this kind of intellectual terror is no picnic. (Today I can appreciate the nineteenth-century freethinker Robert Green Ingersoll's contention that "All the meanness of which the human heart is capable is summed up in that one word—Hell.")

I did what I would always do whenever I was scared and confused. I talked to my mother. My parents had been consistently dedicated to open-mindedness and free inquiry. Though they sent me to church, they never forced their beliefs on me, and they never insisted that I believe in God. If I asked my mother a question or the meaning of a word, rather than provide the answer (which she usually knew), she would instruct me to go to the encyclopedia or to the dictionary for the answer. I was always taught to think for myself and to always ask questions—and most importantly, to demand logical answers to those questions.

My parents never chose my heroes for me. When my father would ask me who my heroes were, I would tell him, and he would bring me literature so that I could learn more about them—whether he approved of them or not. Of course, this kind of parenting does not necessarily make for a good religionist.

I asked my mother how I could be sure which religion—if any— was true. She said that I could never be sure, but that I should examine them all and decide for myself. I then asked her what would happen if I decided not to believe in God at all, and she said she would love me still. From that day forward I never ceased to ask questions and to demand that they be answered logically.

When I was ten years of age, the Black Power movement swept through my Pittsburgh neighborhood in the 1960s. I became increasingly militant and wore the *tikis, dashikis,* Black Power necklaces, red, black, and green buttons, and other symbols of Black pride and unity. I learned the Black Power handshake, and the Black Power chant, and eventually grew an Afro. I also heard the name Malcolm X (who had been assassinated a few years earlier) mentioned a great deal.

The following year I developed a voracious appetite for reading, and I wanted to read my first book—any book. I asked my mother which book I should read, and she gave me her copy of *The Autobiography of Malcolm X* (which is still my all-time favorite book). I also started reading the newspaper *Muhammad Speaks*, which was then the official newspaper of the Nation of Islam. I also read the *Black Panther* newspaper and other militant literature.

I learned that Christianity was used as a weapon against Blacks by White supremacists. I learned that the conquest and enslavement of Africans and their consequent oppression was encouraged—or at least had not been opposed—by most White Western Christians. I learned of the role of religionists in the formation of the Ku Klux Klan, the John Birch Society, and other racist organizations. I learned that, as Martin Luther King Jr. profoundly observed, the most segregated hour in America was on Sunday at 11 A.M. And I learned that Christianity made many Blacks "peaceful, passive, and nonviolent," as Malcolm X pointed out in his famous speech, "Message to the Grass Roots." In the same recorded speech I heard Malcolm accuse King and other civil rights leaders of being "religious Uncle Toms" who were leading (or *misleading*) Blacks into the hands of White supremacists like sheep to the slaughterhouse. I came across numerous passages in Black literature like the following from C. Eric Lincoln's *Black Muslims in America* (1961, p. 78):

> The Bible is the graveyard of my poor people . . . and here I quote another poison addiction to the slavery teaching of the Bible: "Love your enemies, bless them who curse you; pray for those who spitefully use you; him that smiteth thee on the cheek, offer the other cheek; him that (robs) taketh away the cloak, forbid him not to take (away) thy coat also. . . ." The Slavemasters [sic] couldn't have found a better teaching for their protection. (Quoted from Elijah Muhammad's booklet *The Supreme Wisdom*)

I found these criticisms to be very accurate, and my greatest heroes and heroines were Black militants who seemed hostile to Christianity. But I did not reject the Christian faith. After all, the church had been filling my head with nonsense long before I had reached the age of reason, and I was still young. Besides, much of the theology of the Nation of Islam was so ridiculous that even a child had to laugh at it. (But of course, had the Nation been fortunate enough to get to me while I was still very young, I undoubtedly would have believed that crap, too.)

When I was about twelve, my mother allowed my brothers and me to decide whether we still wanted to attend church. Not surprisingly, we happily started enjoying our Sunday mornings with football games, trips to the amusement park, and so forth.

Because I was still a Christian, however, I occasionally went to church. There was a time when I missed a Sunday, though. That week, there was quite a commotion in the church. Many people had claimed that they had seen a church member mysteriously levitate as she became "full of the Holy Ghost." People were supposedly frightened and ran out of the church. Like a typical religious knucklehead, I demanded no evidence and blindly believed their story. I felt cheated. I had missed a genuine miracle! I could not allow that to happen, so like millions of gullible believers all over the world, I lied and said that I, too, had witnessed the great miracle (which is probably what the other church members had done anyway).

I never found out exactly what happened that day—or if anything happened at all. But one thing is certain. None of us ever provided a shred of evidence to support our outrageous claim, which, oddly, made it all the more believable to the other unreasoning Christians.

Some of the young Christians at my church had become very inquisitive. The church lessons often sounded like introductory philosophy of religion classes. Young instructors would ask us to provide evidence for the existence of God. They would ask us how we could be certain that the Bible is infallible. We learned the importance of being able to rationally defend our belief system. We were allowed to ask any question on the topic of theology. This was obviously a refreshing departure from the mindless indoctrination to which we had been previously exposed.

When I was in the seventh grade, we studied *Porgy and Bess* in music class. We learned the song "It Ain't Necessarily So." I loved the lyrics! There is one part in particular I have never been able to forget ("The things that you're liable to read in the Bible, it ain't necessarily so"). The song was filled with references to biblical characters and events. The song expressed skepticism toward biblical stories and claims. It was my first thoughtful exposure to freethought, and it was intellectually stimulating.

After high school, I became a born-again Christian. I gave up cursing, chasing girls, and other "sins." I had played drums since I was very young. I started reading music at age ten, and mastered the twenty-six rudiments. I learned to play marching band music, concert band music, orchestra music, R&B, funk, jazz, gospel, and other genres. After I "found the Lord," however, I declined several offers to play with R&B and funk bands throughout the city of Pittsburgh. I had become disgusted with the way popular Black music had become more and more sexually explicit. (This was before the arrival of Prince on the music scene, and long before hard-core hip-hop.)

I read much religious literature, and I learned that any serious born-again Christian had to read the Bible cover-to-cover at least once. I read it, but obviously I did not think deeply about what I read. (As Thomas Paine wisely observed: "The Bible is the most widely read and least examined book in the world.") I came across blatant contradictions and horrible tales of brutality and genocide. I learned of the bloodthirsty exploits of Moses, Aaron, Joshua, Samuel, Gideon, and other biblical "heroes" that made the Ayatollah Khomeini look like the epitome of tolerance.

Such stories caused me great cognitive dissonance. I would become so upset that I would curse God and put down the Bible for days at a time. But religious leaders always said to simply "trust in the Lord. There are some things we puny human beings simply cannot understand." I would then push the biblical atrocities and other problems to the back of my mind and continue reading.

The hardest part about taking Christianity seriously was trying to eliminate my sexual urge. Unlike promiscuous ministers, I had no interest in using Christianity to attain more sexual partners. Not only was I now committed to sexual abstinence, but I clearly understood that *lust* is a sin. I was in a constant—and losing—battle to expunge impure thoughts from my mind.

I found this problem especially disturbing when I began to read the Song of Solomon. This book of the Bible is highly erotic, and I still cannot understand how it found its way into the "Good Book." King Solomon and the "Black but comely" Queen of Sheba revel in the sexual love they share. I found myself getting sexually excited as I read certain passages, and hoped that the Lord would forgive me for "lusting in my heart" (and elsewhere).

I read *Plain Truth* magazine, published by the Worldwide Church of God. At the time, Herbert Armstrong headed the church. He was adamantly opposed to divorce, though he later divorced his wife. Armstrong's hypocrisy aside, I learned a great deal from his organization's literature. I learned that Christmas, Easter, and other Christian holy days were in reality pagan holidays. They were rooted in pre-Christian religions and cultural practices.

The most important fact that I learned from *Plain Truth* was that the concepts of heaven and hell had their roots in pre-Christian religions. The writers of the magazine persuasively argued that the idea of hell could in no way be reconciled with a belief in a perfectly good God. I gained a great deal of relief after having examined their arguments.

The *Plain Truth*, however, might have been the truth. But it clearly was not the *complete* truth. I later became widely and deeply read in Black history throughout the world. I read the works of J. A. Rogers, Cheikh Anta Diop, John Henrik Clarke, John G. Jackson, and Ivan Van Sertima, as well as noted biblical scholars. I discovered that *Plain Truth* conveniently neglected to discuss the so-called pagan origins of Judaism and Christianity. Long before Christ, there had been saviors born to virgins. They had become wise beyond their years. They had disciples, performed miracles, and were persecuted and resurrected after three days. For example, the Egyptian trinity of Isis, Horus, and Osiris preceded the Christian trinity by centuries.

I had learned that monotheism did not begin with the ancient Hebrews. The pharaoh Akhenaton instituted worship of the sun. Long before the supposed Exodus, he taught that the sun was the only god. The Hebrews, on the other hand, were henotheists. They believed in more than one god, but they claimed that Yahweh was greater than the others ("My God can lick your god.").

The Ten Commandments were not original. The Code of Hammurabi of the Babylonians and the Declarations of Innocence of the

Egyptians were in effect before Moses supposedly arrived on the religion scene. It had become clear to me that morality came about as a result of practical necessity, not divine command. (As Ingersoll put it, "There have always been laws against murder—and there always will be, as long as men object to being murdered.") In short, I learned that Judaism and Christianity have about as much originality as a mimeograph machine.

In college I learned that the Bible is clearly the product of deranged, immoral human beings. In a philosophy class titled "Philosophy of Religion," the instructor called attention to the blatant atrocities, absurdities, inconsistencies, and contradictions of Christianity. I was introduced to the works of Ingersoll, Voltaire, Thomas Paine, Bertrand Russell, and other philosophers and freethinkers. I later became a deist and a freethinker, and there was no looking back. As one atheist put it, trying to embrace religion again is like trying to unlearn the alphabet. I had learned many important truths about the history and practice of Christianity, and I could only go forward in my thinking.

While I was an undergraduate student at the University of Pittsburgh, I embraced Marxism. I read the *Militant* and other Marxist publications and books. I attended many speeches and events sponsored by socialists. I eventually rejected Marxism, however, because I realized that most Americans would never accept it. It sounded great in theory, but it has never worked for the masses in practice. In Marxist nations, the social, political, and economic power is still concentrated in the hands of a small privileged class. In the best of times, "the people" have a little food, but very few luxuries. They have small, cramped housing and no serious homeless problem, but no choice in where they will live. They have low-paying jobs with benefits, but no real career choices. They are literate and educated, but the government determines what they will read, and they have no civil liberties.

My Marxist comrades had always compared the best features of Marxism to the worst aspects of capitalism. Marxism certainly looks better from that perspective. Most humanists, however, do not want to simply exist and be imprisoned by the state in the name of what is best for "the people." We do not simply want the bare necessities. We want to be able to pursue happiness.

Someone once remarked that "immigration is the highest form of flattery." Indeed, millions of people throughout the world try to move to capitalist nations. Not many people in capitalist nations, however, have tried to make it to nations ruled by Marxist governments. This is not because most people have been deceived by capitalist propaganda. It is because they clearly understand that capitalist nations offer them the best chance at happiness.

An old eastern European proverb goes: "Under capitalism, man exploits man. Under communism, the reverse is true." Despite the many problems that we experience in the United States, however, there is always hope and opportunity. Though Black militants such as Marcus Garvey, Malcolm X, and Louis Farrakhan condemn America, in their unguarded moments they marvel at America's democratic practices and potential. Moreover, most Blacks in the United States have never had a desire to live in any other nation. They clearly understand that many conditions for Blacks continue to improve in the United States, and that they would probably be much worse off in most—if not all—other countries.

I have come to prefer the social welfare democracies of Norway, Sweden, Denmark, and other Scandinavian countries. Not all humanists accept this kind of arrangement, however. Some libertarians complain that it is immoral and coercive for a government to take money that its citizens have rightfully earned. Some libertarians believe that the government should exist only to negotiate differences among individuals and organizations, and for purposes of national defense. Some libertarian extremists—like anarchists—believe that there is no need for government.

Humanists might be socialists, communists, or capitalists. I cannot discuss all of these systems in detail in this essay. Humanists, however, believe that we should all participate in free discussions on these matters. Furthermore, we should all keep sufficiently open minds rather than simply try to justify rigidly held beliefs.

In the 1980s I wholeheartedly embraced Afrocentrism. Most Afrocentrists were harsh critics of Judaism, Christianity, and Islam. They noted that while many Black militants recognized that biblical teachings were often used to oppress Black people, they mistakenly believed that Islam was "the Black man's true religion." The historian Chancellor Williams discussed some of the ways in which Islam was used to harm people of African descent in his book *The Destruction of Black Civilization*. Some Rastafarians and others argued that much of Islam was inconsistent with and hostile toward indigenous African religions. Such arguments vastly increased my suspicion of organized religions.

My brother, Dave Allen (a contributor to this volume), pushed me from deistic humanism toward full-fledged atheism and secular humanism. I had read a book titled *An Anthology of Atheism and Rationalism* by the late Gordon Stein (who would later become my colleague). Later I received a catalog from Prometheus Books, and was amazed at the many books they carried on atheism, rationalism, freethought, and humanism. I ordered several books from Prometheus including *The Atheist Debater's Handbook*, by B. C. Johnson, and *Atheism: The Case Against God*, by George H. Smith. After I finished them, I gave them to Dave, and he devoured both of them. His atheism had become complete.

Dave was surprised to learn that I could still believe in God after having read so many devastating critiques of theism. He made me realize that I was simply embracing a God of the gaps. There were two theistic claims that I still found to be very powerful. First, there was the design argument. Second, there were the claims that hundreds of biblical prophecies had been fulfilled. Dave, however, had made me realize that the baby had drowned and the bathwater had become dirty. It was time to throw out the bathwater and bury the rotting corpse of the theistic baby.

I have long since answered these two mysteries to my satisfaction. As a Christian, I had been taught that biblical prophecies are special, because they come from God and are *never* wrong. I learned, however, that most biblical prophecies are so vague that they could apply to almost any event and any point in history. The biblical writers did not give exact dates or times. For example, the Bible says that prior to Christ's return, "there will be wars and rumors of wars." That is a pretty safe prophecy. Indeed, it covers most of human history.

Where specific prophecies are concerned, biblical writers would often interpolate them into the Bible *after* the events had occurred. What is much worse, there are many failed biblical prophecies. For example, in Isa. 17:1 the prophet predicted the imminent destruction of Damascus. But Damascus, the capital of Syria, remains standing to this day.

The most important biblical prophecy has turned out to be the most embarrassing for Christians. Christ promised his original followers that he would return during their lifetimes (Matt. 16:27–28, 24:29–34; Luke 9:26–27, 21:25–32; Mark 9:1; 1 Pet. 4:7; and so forth). This is the granddaddy of all failed prophecies! It is therefore clear that there is nothing impressive or unique about biblical prophecies.

The design argument also fails to stand up to critical examination. Order and design are not one and the same. The theory of evolution by natural selection, neo-Mendelian genetics, the laws of biochemistry, and contemporary cosmology clearly demonstrate that life could have arisen strictly as a result of natural processes. Darwin's theory demonstrates how matter acting in accordance with the natural laws of physics is self-organizing. The laws of physics probably could have come about naturally as the universe began to cool and expand shortly after the occurrence of the big bang.

I had always been impressed by the theological argument that it is highly improbable that life could have arisen without divine intervention. Theologians would claim that it would be just as likely that a tornado could sweep through a junkyard and create an airplane. Others claimed that it would be as unlikely as a chimp sitting at a typewriter and duplicating a work of Shakespeare. They would bandy about impressive, mind-boggling numbers from mathematicians to support their case.

But where were they getting these numbers? As one atheist mathematician has asserted, they must have been grabbing them out of the clear blue sky! Indeed, questions of probability are meaningless unless we have background information to support them. These mathematicians could not possibly know what they claim to know. As David Hume long ago noted, these kinds of claims are false analogies because, as far as we know, there is only one universe. We have no other universe to present in comparison. If we had other universes, we would still have to know how they came about, how life came into existence in all of the other universes, and so forth. The probability of the universe existing is one, as far as we can tell.

Theologians would also claim that the eye is "irreducibly complex," and therefore must be the creation of an intelligent designer. That is not the way the world's top scientists see it, however. In his book *Climbing Mount Improbable*, Richard Dawkins points out that the eye has evolved independently at least forty different times over the past five hundred thousand years.

William Lane Craig is a clever Christian debater. He claims that we *know* that everything that begins to exist in space and time must have a cause. He further asserts that God exists outside space and time, and therefore is in no need of a creator. God has always existed and always will exist. This sounds impressive until we start demanding evidence to support this extraordinary claim. Craig has no evidence that God—or anything else—exists outside space and time. If, however, a mysterious force exists outside space and time, why could it not be a nonrational, quasi-natural force? Why must it be a deity? Moreover, if everything that begins to exist in space and time must have a cause, why could it not be a perfectly *natural* cause?

It is quite clear that the God of today is a God of the gaps. I would rather simply profess ignorance than to try to fill in the gaps in my knowledge by positing a mysterious, unknowable being.

I eventually subscribed to *Free Inquiry* magazine, published by the Council for Secular Humanism. *Free Inquiry* remains the most impressive journal I have ever read on the subject of humanism. Later, I read the *Skeptical Inquirer*, published by the Committee for the Scientific Investigation of Claims of the Paranormal (CSICOP). This journal deals with the examination of such phenomena as UFOs, alien abductions, ghosts, psychics, haunted houses, cryptozoology, and so forth. To a lesser degree, CSICOP is also concerned with bad science, fringe science, pseudoscience, revisionist history, and other subjects. This emphasis upon skeptical inquiry as a methodology influenced my worldview more than any other single idea. I learned to think critically in *all* areas of life. However, I maintained my commitment to truth, fairness, and goodwill toward human beings. Rather than blindly embrace a naïve form of scientism, I would critically examine my worldview with the same relentless honesty with which I would examine all ideas. I would not feel intellectually obligated to rationalize weaknesses in any idea to which I was attracted.

Because I embraced this methodology, I could no longer define myself as an Afrocentrist. There is too much in Afrocentricity that fosters irrationality, pseudoscience, and dubious scholarship. Most Afrocentrists accept or refuse to critique a belief in melaninism, or the idea that the melanin pigment in Blacks makes us superior to Whites. Many Afrocentric scholars accept the idea that ancient Egyptians flew airplanes and practiced telekinesis. Many Afrocentrists have been blatantly sexist, homophobic, and anti-Jewish. They have condemned the idea of church/state separation, and they have assumed many reactionary positions that are not consistent with the notion of universal human rights.

The heroes of my childhood are not necessarily my heroes today. Over the years I learned that members of the Nation of Islam had engaged in many despicable actions, including the assassination of Malcolm X. I leaned that, though the Black Panthers started out as a progressive organization, many of them succumbed to treachery and criminality. Many cultural nationalists that I idolized became drug addicts. I am not disillusioned, however. Nor do I have any desire to ignore, downplay, or rationalize their behavior. I have simply chosen to accept reality and deal with it.

While I was growing up, aside from the Beatles, I had no White heroes or heroines. I have learned, however, that true heroism, wisdom, and greatness are to be found throughout the world among all peoples. Among the many intellectual and activist idols of my childhood, only one remains—Malcolm X. Today, my other heroes include Socrates, Confucius, Ingersoll, Nelson Mandela, the former South African Black Power leader Steve Biko, and the former Congolese freedom fighter Patrice Lumumba. I have learned to be concerned primarily with substance over style and other superficial aspects of one's personality.

Humanism has much to offer the world. Philosophically, there is no problem of evil with which to contend. In the natural world, catastrophes occur and people have the capacity for good and evil. Conversely, most theists are confronted with the unsolvable problem of trying to reconcile their belief in a *perfectly* good God with the existence of evil.

There have been no humanist holy wars. Organized humanists have never disrupted cultures or tried to force everyone to accept their worldview. We have never enslaved people for rejecting humanism. Organized humanists have consistently emphasized the use of reasoned debate to resolve disputes. For these reasons and more, humanism can help to make the world more peaceful and democratic.

Courageous humanists are willing to sufficiently, consistently, and uncompromisingly challenge the numerous ways in which religion harms society. We have the courage and the ethical conviction to follow the arguments wherever they lead. We will oppose faith healing, pedophilia in the clergy, holy wars, patriarchy, sexism, homophobia, slavery, imperialism, genocide, and all other crimes against humanity condoned in the name of God.

Humanists may be called upon to promote good science and medical progress. Many religionists have retarded success in these areas. The church opposed the use of cadavers for medical research. It opposed the use of anesthesia for women during childbirth. It opposed vaccination against disease. Some religionists oppose blood transfusions, organ transplants, and other medical procedures for extending and improving human lives.

Two of the biggest controversies of the early part of the new millennium surround AIDS prevention and stem cell research. Catholic leaders in southern Africa are debating whether to lift the ban on condoms in a belated effort to combat AIDS. Islamic nations are opposed to a United Nations global AIDS plan to "promote and protect the health" of gays, prostitutes, drug addicts, and other high-risk groups. These religionists are more obsessed with their own sense of morality than they are with saving lives. Their views help to *increase* the spread of AIDS. Humanists, on the other hand, are primarily concerned with ideas and consequences and how they impact upon the lives of human beings. That is to say, humanists place the welfare of humanity above blind obedience to tradition and ossified religious opinions.

On the issue of stem cell research, practically everyone agrees that the controversy surrounds whether the destruction of an embryo is murder. It is quite a stretch, however, to equate an embryo with a human being. It is like arguing that an acorn is an oak tree, or that a seed is a flower. Many religionists, though, are concerned about what will happen to the embryo's supposed soul. This is odd, to say the least. A reasonable person would conclude that, because a microscopic embryo does not have a body or a mind, it is reasonably certain that it has no soul. In any case, hundreds of thousands of stem cells will be discarded. Millions of embryos are discarded naturally all over the world every month. It is just too bad that religion is often impervious to reason and common sense.

There are many possible medical uses for stem cells. They might be used to treat stroke, cancer, diabetes, heart attack, multiple sclerosis, liver disease, Parkinson's disease, Alzheimer's disease, blood, bone, and bone marrow ailments, and more. Some believe that scientists might be able to create organs and provide skin grafts for severe burn patients. Researchers in Israel have reported that they were able to get embryonic stem cells to create heart-muscle cells, which they saw beating in a laboratory dish. In another experiment, researchers found that mice with a type of Parkinson's disease were cured after transformed cells began producing a missing chemical.

Though reactionary theists claim the moral high ground in this debate, outspoken humanists will continue to assertively fight for the rights of suffering patients. Rather than cowardly concede the moral high ground to quietistic religious leaders, humanists maintain that it is unethical to prevent medical and technological research that could be used to cure diseases.

Humanism could produce a consistently humane and ethical vision for society. As Eleanor Roosevelt wisely observed, democracy requires eternal vigilance. Many people, however, take their civil liberties for granted. Furthermore, whenever people are struggling, they often embrace antidemocratic ideas, leaders, organizations, and institutions. They become so intensely obsessed with the problems that afflict them that they are willing to risk all of their freedoms by succumbing to the charms of charismatic demagogues filled with empty promises.

Humanism, however, stresses the importance of critical thinking, ethical conduct, and democracy. Ethical humanists are not simply concerned with eliminating injustice. Just as importantly, we are concerned with implementing *democratic* solutions. We are able to identify progressive-sounding ideas masked behind reactionary and fascist agendas and worldviews. We hate all kinds of injustice but love justice even more.

Humanists are opposed to irrationality and misology. We are skeptical of untested claims to knowledge such as those put forth by paranoid conspiracy theorists. For example, many people believe that the U.S. Air Force is withholding proof that extraterrestrial aliens have visited Earth.

According to an article on page A2 of the July 15, 1997, issue of the *Washington Times*, the Scripps Howard News Service, the E. W. Scripps School of Journalism, and Ohio University conducted a poll of 1,009 people. The poll found that "people of every race, age, education level, economic status and political orientation believe in government conspiracy theories." Those most likely to believe are Blacks, poor people, and young people. The conspiracy theories that the poll covered included claims like those about UFOs, as well as claims like those concerning the belief that military leaders were hiding information about the use of nerve gas during the Persian Gulf War.

While skepticism of untested claims to knowledge might be a virtue, burying one's head in the sand is not. Thoughtful humanists will carefully examine conspiracy claims before accepting or rejecting them. Because in reality, military leaders, political leaders, and government agencies are not nearly as benign as many skeptics seem to believe.

One reason why conspiracy theories are so attractive to so many people is that genuine conspiracies have taken place. Perhaps the most famous conspiracy is the Tuskegee experiment in which hundreds of Black men were allowed to go untreated with syphilis from the 1930s until the experiment ended in the 1970s. (Former President Clinton apologized to survivors.) For years many White skeptics ignored the atrocity. Today many skeptics dismiss it as a mere aberration.

This was no mere aberration, however. Clinton also apologized for the thousands of radioactive experiments that the government carried out on Americans beginning in the 1940s. The United States, however, is not the only nation to engage in conspiratorial behavior.

__IMG0__

According to the August 26, 1997, issue of the *Arizona Daily Star*, the Swedish government sterilized sixty thousand "inferior" people between 1935 and 1976—some of them by force. Among them were people with poor vision, mental retardation, or "undesirable" racial characteristics. The program was the result of an effort to improve human beings through eugenics.

There are extremists among skeptics. Some people misapply skepticism as a rationalization for ignoring uncomfortable truths. Responsible humanists, however, stress the importance of being reasonably skeptical of untested claims to knowledge. We further recognize the importance of openness to new ideas and new information. We will acknowledge and combat the diabolical actions of government leaders and organizations without fostering a consistently paranoid mind-set.

It does not matter whether God exists. Any good that God is able or willing to do is insignificant compared to what we human beings must do for ourselves. Our history clearly demonstrates this simple fact. The abolition of slavery came about because *human beings* spoke, wrote, organized, and fought for freedom. There is no evidence that any guardian angels were involved in the warfare.

Similarly, the success of the civil rights movement can be explained in terms that are clearly and strictly human. Human beings spoke, sang, organized, and marched to bring about positive change. Again, there is no evidence that divine intervention played any role in the success of that struggle. There were no religious miracles performed at the March on Washington, in Selma, in Montgomery, and so forth.

To paraphrase Albert Camus, we are condemned to be humanists. Genuine progress and widespread happiness come about when we are able and willing to place the needs of humanity at the center of our existence. We must never forget, however, that we are human and imperfect. We are apt to make mistakes—even huge blunders—in our attempts to improve society. After all, there is no perfect God to guide us. Unlike religious extremists, though, we must not be afraid to experiment socially, politically, economically, ethically, and scientifically. We must always consider the possible consequences of our ideas and actions. We must then proceed with caution if we collectively determine that present conditions are unfair, inhumane, or intolerable. Progress always comes with an element of risk—and sometimes danger.

We have much work to do. We will courageously move forward or we will give in to despair. Confident humanists refuse to give up. We will move forward and we will do much good in the world. In the words of Confucius, "It is better to light one candle than to curse the darkness."

...much work to do....

...a Constitution. This brief account...

CONTRIBUTORS

DAVID ALLEN is the brother of editor Norm R. Allen Jr. and is an advisory board member of African Americans for Humanism. He lives and works in Prince George's County, Maryland.

ANTHONY BURNSIDE is a magician from Kansas City, Missouri. He has demonstrated how "psychic" surgeons from the Philippines trick desperate people into paying for their services.

CAROLYN M. DEJOIE is a professor emerita at the University of Wisconsin-Madison. She is a secular humanist activist and is interested in establishing a humanist group in the Madison area.

CHARLES W. FAULKNER is a syndicated columnist and a psychologist. His column has appeared in hundreds of Black newspapers throughout North America. He is a contributing editor to *Free Inquiry*.

CHAKA FERGUSON is a journalist for the Associated Press and lives in Irvington, New Jersey.

LEONARD HARRIS is currently a Distinguished Visiting Professor at William Patterson University in Wayne, New Jersey. He is one of the world's leading scholars on the life and philosophy of Alain Locke, and a leader of the Philosophy Born of Struggle Association, which hosts annual conferences on Locke. His books include *The Philosophy of Alain Locke* and *Racism*.

GLADMAN C. HUMBLES was the first Black firefighter in Paducah, Kentucky, and the first Black president of the international firefighters union. He has received two awards for outstanding leadership as the president of the Paducah NAACP. He has performed as a magician and has written several newspaper articles.

LEO IGWE is the secretary of the Nigerian Humanist Movement and the chairperson of the Center for Inquiry-Nigeria.

PATRICK INNISS is a former vice president of the Rationalist Society of St. Louis and an advisory board member of African Americans for Humanism. He is a former columnist for the *Secular Humanist Press,* the newsletter of the Humanists of Washington.

ALFRED T. KISUBI is a poet and a philosopher. He is a Distinguished and Full Professor of Education and Human Services at the University of Wisconsin-Oshkosh. He is a member of the editorial board of *Free Inquiry* magazine.

MICAH LAMPTEY is a member of the Rational Centre headquartered in Accra, Ghana.

DOMINIC I. OGBONNA is a philosopher and a leader of the Nigerian Humanist Movement.

KEENYA H. OLIVER is from Glen Ellyn, Illinois.

NKEONYE OTAKPOR is a professor emeritus at the Department of Philosophy at the University of Benin in Nigeria.

ANTHONY B. PINN is an assistant professor of religious studies at Macalester College in St. Paul, Minnesota. He is a member of the editorial board of *Free Inquiry* magazine. He is the author of several books including *Why, Lord?* and *Varieties of African American Religious Experience.*

DAVID STEWART SUMMERS is a writer and a physician with a practice in Erie, Pennsylvania.

RANJINI L. THAVER is an associate professor of economics at Stetson University in DeLand, Florida.

IGWE UCHEAKOLAM is an environmental activist and a member of the Nigerian Humanist Movement headquartered in Ibadan, Nigeria.

FRANZ VANDERPUYE is a journalist and a humanist activist in Ghana.

KENYATTA YAMEL is a progressive activist and a freelance writer from Milwaukee, Wisconsin.

GEBREGEORGIS YOHANNES is the president of the Ethiopian Humanist Organization. He is a leader of the African Humanist Alliance and hosts a Web site commemorating the life and work of Patrice Lumumba, the first prime minister of the Congo.